RUSSELL ASH

Over 250 lists that matter!

RUSSELL ASH

TOP 10 FOR MEN

Over 250 lists that matter!

hamlyn

An Hachette UK Company
www.hachette.co.uk

First published in Great Britain in 2010 by
Hamlyn, a division of Octopus Publishing Group Ltd
Endeavour House, 189 Shaftesbury Avenue, London WC2H 8JY
www.octopusbooksusa.com

Distributed in the U.S. and Canada by Octopus Books USA:
c/o Hachette Book Group
237 Park Avenue
New York, NY 10017

ISBN 978-0-600-62070-9

Printed and bound in China

10 9 8 7 6 5 4 3 2

CONTENTS

INTRODUCTION

It's a guy thing...

A number of books try to explain the differences—aside from the obvious ones—between the sexes, hence books with titles like *Why Men Don't Listen and Women Can't Read Maps* (no problem, now that we all have SatNav) and *Men Are from Mars, Women Are from Venus* (what's that all about?). This book has no such pretensions: it simply accepts the fact that men like lists, so here's a selection of over 250 lists that you—assuming that you are a man—may enjoy. They encompass themes ranging from music to sports, from the fastest—and the most stolen, and most expensive —cars to the hottest chilies and the players with most home runs. There are many even more offbeat ones: the deadliest creatures; the biggest movie flops; the most dangerous snakes, sharks, and causes of home accidents; the mammals with the highest sperm count (sorry to have to break it to you, but we don't feature); plus lists of preserved American bodies and body parts; people who died while performing; and winners of the "worst dressed."

Nothing like a Dame

OK, plenty of women make lists (I am married to one of them), but they are shopping lists, lists of tasks for themselves or their partners to do around the home, and suchlike, not the sort of lists we men like. As the compiler of the annual *Top 10 of Everything* for more than 20 years, I was once invited to appear on a radio show along with the British actress Dame Judi Dench (best known as "M" in the James Bond movies), who a researcher had spotted was an inveterate list compiler. The perfect team, she assumed—except my lists tend to be things like "10 tallest buildings" and "10 fastest jets," while Dame Judi's consisted of "buy shoes" and "go to theater." And was it not Bridget Jones whose list of New Year's resolutions ends with "Stop making lists"? The defense rests...

Men of influence

There are only slightly more men on the planet (3,620,540,003 of us, in 2010, compared with 3,584,516,606 women), but, for better or for worse, men are hugely disproportionate in terms of influence and hence prominence in Top 10 lists. As they reveal, the richest people are all men, as are the highest-earning sportsmen—obviously, as they are men, but I gave up trying to compile a Top 10 of richest sportswomen since, after Maria Sharapova, Serena Williams, Michelle Wie, and Annika Sorenstam, you are struggling. Every land, air, and water speed record has been held by a man. All the most expensive paintings are by men, and the Top 10 items of rock memorabilia relate to male stars—it's not quite the same with film memorabilia, but we can guess what sort of men would pay serious money for Judy Garland's ruby slippers from *The Wizard of Oz*. Throwing a discus is the only notable sport in which the woman's record is greater than a man's—but then a woman's discus is half the weight of the man's. We are also the guys who brought you the wars, the mass murders, and other fun stuff: hence the lists of air aces (not a gal among them) and worst serial killers (all men)—although, to redress the balance, there's a list of the 10 worst murderesses.

Trivia, not trivial

When I was a boy (I never thought I'd say that, but there comes a point in a guy's life when he's entitled to do so), we used to call our expansive knowledge of the world around us "general knowledge." Somehow, in recent years, this has been subverted and is now known as "trivia," as though it's somehow trivial. Well, it isn't: either you are interested in what's happening, or you aren't, and if you are not, it's your loss. Fortunately, most men—not just nerds—are deeply interested in everything; it's just that we don't want to waste our time discriminating between crucial information, like what are the world's largest countries, and even more crucial stuff, such as the best-selling albums. Without this data at our fingertips, we couldn't polish off crossword puzzles, hold our own in quizzes, or answer all the questions on *Who Wants to be a Millionaire?* faster than the contestants in the hot seats.

Size is everything

...at least when it comes to Top 10 lists. When I started compiling *Top 10 of Everything*, back in the mists of time (OK, 1989), I gave myself the task of including only quantifiable lists. I figured that if I could measure it (biggest, fastest, oldest, or whatever), and I did my research correctly, the lists could not be challenged—unlike a list of 10 favorites or bests, where my authority to make such a claim might reasonably be questioned. So, aside from an occasional lapse (it's allowed, I wrote it), most of the lists here are of things that can be measured and hence ranked—movie lists are mostly ordered by global box office earnings, death and destruction lists by fatalities. So, unlike certain other books, instead of just being told what's at the top of the tree, you get to explore its lower branches. And didn't you always want to know who came in second?

Who says so?

I use a diverse range of international organizations, commercial companies, research bodies, specialized publications, and a number of experts around the world, whom I thank collectively (see page 287–288 for a full list of credits).

1	R
2	U
3	S
4	S
5	E
6	L
7	L
8	A
9	S
10	H

Please send me any comments (or corrections, if you must) and ideas for lists to the official *Top 10* site—www.top10ofeverything.com or to me personally at my website www.RussellAsh.com

HIGHEST MOUNTAINS CLIMBED SINCE THE CONQUEST OF EVEREST*

	Mountain	First ascent	Height
1	K2	Jul 31, 1954	28,251 ft (8,611 m)
2	Kangchenjunga	May 25, 1955	28,169 ft (8,586 m)
3	Lhotse	May 18, 1956	27,940 ft (8,516 m)
4	Makalu	May 15, 1955	27,762 ft (8,462 m)
5	Cho Oyu	Oct 19, 1954	26,906 ft (8,201 m)
6	Dhaulagri	May 13, 1960	26,794 ft (8,167 m)
7	Manaslu	May 9, 1956	26,759 ft (8,156 m)
8	Nanga Parbat	Jul 3, 1953	26,660 ft (8,126 m)
9	Gasherbrum I	Jul 5, 1958	26,509 ft (8,080 m)
10	Broad Peak	Jun 9, 1957	26,400 ft (8,047 m)

* 29,028 ft (8,848 m); first climbed May 29, 1953

DEEPEST CAVES

	Cave system/location	Depth
1	Krubera (Voronja), Georgia	7,188 ft (2,191 m)
2	Illyuzia-Mezhonnogo-Snezhnaya, Georgia	5,751 ft (1,753 m)
3	Lamprechtsofen Vogelschacht Weg Schacht, Austria	5,354 ft (1,632 m)
4	Gouffre Mirolda, France	5,335 ft (1,626 m)
5	Réseau Jean Bernard, France	5,256 ft (1,602 m)
6	Torca del Cerro del Cuevon/ Torca de las Saxifragas, Spain	5,213 ft (1,589 m)
7	Sarma, Georgia	5,062 ft (1,543 m)
8	Shakta Vjacheslav Pantjukhina, Georgia	4,948 ft (1,508 m)
9	Sima de la Conisa/Torca Magali, Spain	4,944 ft (1,507 m)
10	Cehi 2, Slovenia	4,928 ft (1,502 m)

The world's deepest cave is a comparatively recent discovery: in January 2001 a team of Ukrainian cave explorers in the Arabikskaja system in the western Caucasus mountains of the Georgian Republic found a branch of the Voronja or "Crow's Cave" and established that its depth of 5,610 ft (1,710 m) far exceeded anything previously known. Progressively deeper penetrations have taken its extent to almost seven times the height of the Eiffel Tower. America's deepest cave is the Kazumura Cave, Hawaii, at 3,614 ft (1,102 m).

THE 10
WORST EARTHQUAKES

	Location	Date	Estimated number killed
1	Near East/Mediterranean	May 20, 1202	1,100,000
2	Shenshi, China	Feb 2, 1556	820,000
3	Calcutta, India	Oct 11, 1737	300,000
4	Antioch, Syria	May 20, 526	250,000
5	Tang-shan, China	Jul 28, 1976	242,419
6	Nan-Shan, China	May 22, 1927	200,000
7	Yeddo, Japan	Dec 30, 1703	190,000
8	Kansu, China	Dec 16, 1920	180,000
9	Messina, Italy	Dec 28, 1908	160,000
10	Tokyo/Yokohama, Japan	Sep 1, 1923	142,807

There are often discrepancies between the "official" death tolls in many of the world's worst earthquakes and the estimates given by other authorities: for example, a figure of 750,000 is sometimes quoted for the Tang-shan earthquake of 1976. Several other earthquakes in China and Turkey resulted in the deaths of 100,000 or more. In recent times, the Armenian earthquake of December 7, 1988, and that which struck northwest Iran on June 21, 1990, caused the deaths of more than 55,000 (official estimate: 28,854) and 50,000 respectively. The famous earthquake that destroyed San Francisco on April 18, 1906, killed between 500 and 1,000, mostly in the fires that followed the shock. The earthquake that struck Kobe, Japan (now officially known as the Hyougo-ken Nanbu earthquake), at 5:46 a.m. on January 17, 1995, was exceptionally precisely monitored by the rescue authorities and indicates the severity of an earthquake affecting a densely populated urban area. It left 3,842 dead and 14,679 injured. A further 114,679 people were immediately evacuated, the total rising by January 26 to 232,403. Reaching 7.2 on the Richter scale, the initial shock completely destroyed 54,949 buildings and damaged a further 31,783, while the fires that followed devastated an area of 162.72 acres (65.85 hectares), including 7,377 buildings.

THE 10
WORST EPIDEMICS

	Epidemic	Location	Date	Estimated number killed
1	Black Death	Europe/Asia	1347–80s	75,000,000
2	Influenza	Worldwide	1918–20	20–40,000,000
3	AIDS	Worldwide	1981–	>25,000,000
4	Plague of Justinian	Europe/Asia	541–90	<25,000,000
5	Bubonic plague	India	1896–1948	12,000,000
6	Antonine plague (probably smallpox)	Roman Empire	165–80	5,000,000
7	Typhus	Eastern Europe	1918–22	3,000,000
8=	Smallpox	Mexico	1530–45	>1,000,000
=	Cholera	Russia	1852–60	>1,000,000
10	Plague of Orosius*	Roman Empire	125	1,000,000

*So called, as it was described by 5th-century historian Paulus Orosius

Precise figures for deaths during the disruptions of epidemics are inevitably unreliable, but the Black Death, or bubonic plague, probably transmitted by fleas from infected rats, swept across Asia and Europe in the 14th century, destroying entire populations, including more than half the inhabitants of London, some 25 million in Europe, and 50 million in Asia.

THE 10
WORST VOLCANIC ERUPTIONS

Location	Date	Estimated number killed
1 Tambora, Indonesia	Apr 5–12, 1815	**92,000**

It has been calculated that between 1600 and 1982 a total of 160,783 people lost their lives as a result of volcanoes in Indonesia, the greatest for any region in the world. The cataclysmic eruption of Tambora on the island of Sumbawa killed about 10,000 islanders immediately, with a further 82,000 dying subsequently (38,000 on Sumbawa and 44,000 on neighboring Lombok) from disease and famine because crops were destroyed. An estimated 1.9 million tons (1.7 million tonnes) of ash were hurled into the atmosphere. This blocked out the sunlight and affected the weather over large areas of the globe during the following year. One effect of this was to produce brilliantly colored sunsets, as depicted strikingly in paintings from the period, especially in the works of British artist J. M. W. Turner. It even influenced literary history when, kept indoors by inclement weather at the Villa Diodati on Lake Geneva, Switzerland, poet Lord Byron and his companions amused themselves by writing horror stories, one of which was Mary Shelley's classic, *Frankenstein*.

2 Krakatoa, Sumatra/Java	Aug 26–27, 1883	**36,380**

After a series of eruptions over the course of several days, the uninhabited island of Krakatoa exploded with what may have been the biggest bang ever heard by humans, audible up to 3,000 miles (4,800 km) away. Some sources put the fatalities as high as 200,000, most of them killed by subsequent tsunamis that reached 100 ft (30 m) high. The events were portrayed in the 1969 movie *Krakatoa, East of Java*—though purists should note that Krakatoa is actually *west* of Java.

3 Mont Pelée, Martinique	May 8, 1902	**27,000**

After lying dormant for centuries, Mont Pelée began to erupt in April 1902. Assured that there was no danger, the residents of the main city, St. Pierre, stayed in their homes and were there when, at 7:30 a.m. on May 8, the volcano burst apart and showered the port with molten lava, ash, and gas, destroying virtually all life and property. Among the survivors, Louis-Auguste Sylbaris, a prisoner in St. Pierre jail, later joined Barnum and Bailey's circus as "The Amazing Survivor of Mont Pelée."

4   Nevado del Ruiz,   Nov 13, 1985   **22,940**
     Colombia
     The Andean volcano gave warning signs of erupting, but by the time it was
     decided to evacuate the local inhabitants, it was too late. The hot steam, rocks,
     and ash ejected from Nevado del Ruiz melted its ice cap, resulting in a mudslide
     that completely engulfed the town of Armero.

5   Mount Etna, Sicily   Mar 11, 1669   **up to 20,000**
     Europe's largest volcano (10,760 ft/3,280 m) has erupted frequently, but the
     worst instance occurred in 1669, when the lava flow engulfed the town of
     Catania, according to some accounts killing as many as 20,000.

6   Mount Etna, Sicily   1169   **over 15,000**
     Large numbers died in Catania Cathedral, where they believed they would be
     safe, and more were killed when a tsunami caused by the eruption hit the port of
     Messina.

7   Unzen, Japan   Apr 1, 1792   **14,300**
     During a period of intense volcanic activity in the area, the island of Unzen (or
     Unsen) completely disappeared, killing all its inhabitants.

8   Laki, Iceland   Jan–Jun 1783   **9,350**
     Iceland is one the most volcanically active places on Earth, but because it is
     sparsely populated, eruptions seldom result in major loss of life. The worst
     exception occurred at the Laki volcanic ridge, culminating on June 11 with the
     largest ever recorded lava flow. It engulfed many villages in a river of lava up to
     50 miles (80 km) long and 100 ft (30 m) deep, releasing poisonous gases that
     killed those who managed to escape.

9   Kelut, Indonesia   May 19, 1919   **5,110**
     Dormant since 1901, Kelut (aka Kelud) erupted without warning, ejecting a
     crater lake that killed inhabitants by drowning or in resultant mudslides. The
     volcano remains active, erupting as recently as 2008.

10   Galunggung, Indonesia   Oct 8, 1882   **4,011**
     Galunggung erupted suddenly, spewing boiling mud, burning sulfur, ash, and
     rocks before finally exploding, destroying a total of 114 villages. A further
     eruption in 1982 killed 68 people.

THE 10
WORST FLOODS

	Location	Date	Estimated number killed
1	Huang He River, China	Aug 1931	3,700,000
2	Huang He River, China	Spring 1887	1,500,000
3	Holland	Nov 1, 1530	400,000
4	Kaifong, China	1642	300,000
5	Henan, China	Sep–Nov 1939	>200,000
6	Bengal, India	1876	200,000
7	Yangtze River, China	Aug–Sep 1931	140,000
8	Holland	1646	110,000
9	North Vietnam	Aug 30, 1971	>100,000
10=	Friesland, Holland	1228	100,000
=	Dordrecht, Holland	Apr 16, 1421	100,000
=	Yangtze River, China	Sep 1911	100,000
=	Canton, China	Jun 12, 1915	100,000

Records of floods caused by China's Huang He (or Yellow) River date back to 2297 BC. Since then, it has flooded at least 1,500 times, resulting in millions of deaths and giving it the nickname "China's Sorrow." According to some accounts, the flood of 1887 may have resulted in as many as 6 million deaths, as over 2,000 towns and villages were inundated. In modern times, an extensive program of damming and dyke-building has reduced the danger. Nevertheless, in the 10 years from 1999 to 2008 a high proportion of the estimated worldwide totals of 85,937 people killed and 1,037,953,000 affected by floods were Chinese.

FIRST EXPEDITIONS TO REACH THE NORTH POLE OVERLAND*

	Name[†]/country	Date
1	Ralph S. Plaisted, USA	Apr 19, 1968
2	Wally W. Herbert, UK	Apr 5, 1969
3	Naomi Uemura, Japan	May 1, 1978
4	Dmitri Shparo, USSR	May 31, 1979
5	Sir Ranulph Fiennes/Charles Burton, UK	Apr 11, 1982
6	Will Steger/Paul Schurke, USA	May 1, 1986
7	Jean-Louis Etienne, France	May 11, 1986
8	Fukashi Kazami, Japan	Apr 20, 1987
9	Helen Thayer, USA[‡]	Apr 20, 1988
10	Robert Swan, UK	May 14, 1989

*Confirmed only
†Expedition leader or coleader
‡New Zealand-born

These expeditions—which discount those that are disputed, such as those of rival American explorers Frederick Cook and Robert Peary in 1909—used a variety of methods to reach the Pole. Plaisted's used snowmobiles, Herbert's sled, Shparo's was on skis. Sir Ranulph Fiennes's expedition, with snowmobiles, was the first to reach both the South (Dec 17, 1980) and North Poles. Etienne's was the first solo, on skis, and that of Helen Thayer, aged 50, the first solo female conquest of the Pole. Kazami undertook his journey on a 250-cc motorcycle and Swan was first to reach both Poles on foot.

DEADLIEST SNAKES

Snake/Latin name	Estimated lethal dose for humans (mg)	Potential humans killed per bite	Average venom per bite (mg)
1 Coastal taipan (*Oxyuranus scutellatus*)	1	120	120
2 Common krait (*Bungarus caeruleus*)	0.5	42	84
3 Philippine cobra (*Naja naja philippinensis*)	2	120	60
4= King cobra (*Ophiophagus hannah*)	20	1,000	50
= Russell's viper (*Daboia russelli*)	3	150	50
6 Black mamba (*Dendroaspis polyepis*)	3	135	45
7 Yellow-jawed tommygoff (*Bothrops asper*)	25	1,000	40
8= Multibanded krait (*Bungarus multicinctus*)	0.8	28	35
= Tiger snake (*Notechis scutatus*)	1	35	35
10 Jararacussu (*Bothrops jarararcussu*)	25	800	32

Source: Russell E. Gough

10
DEADLY CREATURES

1   Candiru
Found in South American rivers, they can enter a man's body via his penis, and, unless surgically removed, cause painful death.

2   Electric eel
Freshwater electric eels can discharge up to 650 volts, enough to kill a human.

3   Mosquito
Mosquito-borne malaria has killed more people than any other disease.

4   Piranha
Living in the rivers of South America, these small but incredibly ferocious fish can strip an animal to the bone in minutes.

5   Golden poison frog
Used to tip arrows, the poison from this native of Colombia is sufficient to kill 10 to 20 adults.

6   Japanese puffer
An expensive delicacy in Japan, if they are incorrectly prepared the powerful nerve poison they contain has no known antidote.

7   Scorpion
Scorpions are capable of inflicting painful stings, but seldom cause death in healthy adults.

8   Sea wasp
Also known as box jellyfish, the sea wasp has tentacles up to 30 ft (9 m) long. Its venom can cause death within three minutes.

9   Stingray
Although they rarely kill, Australian naturalist Steve Irwin died when one pierced his heart.

10   Tiger
In India, a tigress known as the "Champawat man-eater" killed a record 436 people before she was shot in 1907 by British big-game hunter Jim Corbett.

MOST COMMON ANIMAL PHOBIAS

	Animal	Medical term
1	Spiders	Arachnophobia or arachnephobia
2	Snakes	Ophidiophobia, ophiophobia, ophiciophobia, herpetophobia or snakephobia
3	Wasps	Spheksophobia
4	Birds (especially pigeons)	Ornithophobia
5	Mice	Musophobia or muriphobia
6	Fish	Ichthyophobia
7	Bees	Apiphobia or apiophobia
8	Dogs	Cynophobia or kynophobia
9	Caterpillars and other insects	Entomophobia
10	Cats	Ailurophobia, Elurophobia, Felinophobia, Galeophobia, Gatophobia

A phobia is a morbid fear that is out of all proportion to the object of the fear. Phobias directed at creatures that may bite, sting, or carry disease, such as rabid dogs or rats during the Plague, are understandable. Such fears are so widespread that they have been readily exploited in movies, including *Snakes on a Plane* (2006), *Arachnophobia* (1990), *The Swarm* (1978), and *The Birds* (1963).

TYPES OF SHARK THAT HAVE KILLED THE MOST HUMANS

	Shark species	Unprovoked attacks*	Fatalities†
1	Great white	237	65
2	Tiger	88	27
3	Bull	82	25
4	Requiem	39	7
5	Blue	13	4
6	Sand tiger	32	3
7	Blacktip	28	1
8	Shortfin mako	8	1
9	Oceanic whitetip	5	1
10	Dusky	3	1

*1580–2008
†Where fatalities are equal, entries are ranked by total attacks
Source: International Shark Attack File, Florida Museum of Natural History

Out of 52 species of shark, these are the only ones on record as having actually killed humans. A total of 672 attacks resulted in 137 fatalities.

HEAVIEST SALTWATER FISH CAUGHT

	Fish/scientific name	Angler/location/date	Weight
1	Great white shark (*Carcharodon carcharias*)	Alfred Dean, Ceduna, South Australia, Apr 21, 1959	**2,664 lb (1,208.38 kg)**
2	Tiger shark (*Galeocerdo cuvier*)	Kevin James Clapson, Ulladulla, Australia, Mar 28, 2004	**1,785 lb 11 oz (809.98 kg)**
3	Greenland shark (*Somniosus microcephalus*)	Terje Nordtvedt, Trondheimsfjord, Norway, Oct 18, 1987	**1,708 lb 9 oz (774.99 kg)**
4	Black marlin (*Istiompax marlina*)	Alfred C. Glassell Jr., Cabo Blanco, Peru, Aug 4, 1953	**1,560 lb (707.61 kg)**
5	Bluefin tuna (*Thunnus thynnus*)	Ken Fraser, Aulds Cove, Nova Scotia, Canada, Oct 26, 1979	**1,496 lb (678.58 kg)**
6	Atlantic blue marlin (*Makaira nigricans*)	Paulo Amorim, Vitoria, Brazil, Feb 29, 1992	**1,402 lb 2 oz (636.99 kg)**

7	Pacific blue marlin (*Makaira nigricans*)	Jay W. de Beaubien, Kaaiwi Point, Kona, Hawaii, USA, May 31, 1982	**1,376 lb** **(624.14 kg)**
8	Sixgill shark (*Hexanchus griseus*)	Clemens Rump, Ascension Island, Nov 21, 2002	**1,298 lb** **(588.76 kg)**
9	Great hammerhead shark (*Sphyrna mokarran*)	Bucky Dennis, Boca Grande, Florida, USA, May 23, 2006	**1,280 lb** **(580.60 kg)**
10	Shortfin mako shark (*Isurus oxyrinchus*)	Luke Sweeney, Chatham, Massachusetts, USA, Jul 21, 2001	**1,221 lb** **(553.84 kg)**

Source: International Game Fish Association

Alfred Dean hooked his world record shark, the largest fish ever caught with rod and line, in just 50 minutes using a 130-lb (59-kg) line. He also caught other great whites weighing 2,536 and 2,333 lb (1,153 and 1,060 kg) . The largest fish caught by an American was the marlin by Alfred C. Glassell, Jr. (1913–2008). Film footage of his record catch was used in the movie *The Old Man and the Sea* (1958), based on the novel by Ernest Hemingway, and material relating to it is displayed in the "Mighty Marlin" exhibit at the IGFA Fishing Hall of Fame & Museum, Dania Beach, Florida.

HEAVIEST FRESHWATER FISH CAUGHT

	Fish/scientific name	Angler/location/date	Weight
1	White sturgeon (*Acipenser transmontanus*)	Joey Pallotta III, Benicia, California, Jul 9, 1983	468 lb (212.28 kg)
2	Alligator gar (*Atractosteus spatula*)	Bill Valverde, Rio Grande, Texas, Dec 2, 1951	279 lb (126.55 kg)
3	Nile perch (*Lates niloticus*)	William Toth, Lake Nasser, Egypt, Dec 20, 2000	230 lb (104.33 kg)
4	Beluga sturgeon (*Huso huso*)	Ms. Merete Lehne, Guryev, Kazakhstan, May 3, 1993	224 lb 13 oz (101.97 kg)
5	Mekong giant catfish (*Pangasianodon gigas*)	Rob Maylin, Gillhams Fishing Resort, Thailand, May 28, 2008	185 lb 2 oz (83.97 kg)
6	Blue catfish (*Ictalurus furcatus*)	Timothy E. Pruitt, Mississippi River, Alton, Illinois, May 21, 2005	124 lb (56.25 kg)

7	Flathead catfish (*Pylodictis olivaris*)	Ken Paulie, Elk City Reservoir, Kansas, May 14, 1998	**123 lb** (55.79 kg)
8	Redtail catfish (*Phractocephalus hemioliopteru*)	Gilberto Fernandes, Rio Amazonas, Brazil, Dec 28, 2008	**121 lb 4 oz** (55 kg)
9	Chinook salmon (*Oncorhynchus tshawytscha*)	Les Anderson, Kenai River, Alaska, May 17, 1985	**97 lb 4 oz** (44.20 kg)
10	Giant tigerfish (*Hydrocynus goliath*)	Raymond Houtmans, Zaire River, Kinshasa, Zaire (now Democratic Republic of the Congo), Jul 9, 1988	**97 lb** (44 kg)

Source: International Game Fish Association

On May 1, 2005, a team of five anglers on the Mekong River, Thailand, caught a Mekong giant catfish weighing 646 lb (293 kg), making it the largest freshwater fish ever, but it has not been ratified by the International Game Fish Association, so the entry at No. 5, at a little over a third the size, is considered the official record-holder. The sturgeon caught by 21-year-old Joey Pallotta III was 9 ft (2.74 m) long; as it is now illegal to keep a fish over 6 ft (1.83 m) in length, the record will probably never be broken.

PEDIGREE DOG
BREEDS IN THE USA

1   Labrador retriever
2   Yorkshire terrier
3   German shepherd
4   Golden retriever
5   Beagle
6   Boxer
7   Dachshund
8   Bulldog
9   Poodle
10   Shih Tzu

Source: The American Kennel Club, 2008

TOP 10

DOGS' NAMES
IN THE USA*

1   Max
2   Jake
3   Buddy
4   Maggie
5   Bear
6   Molly
7   Bailey
8   Shadow
9   Sam
10 Lady

*Based on a survey of the most popular names on pet identification tags

DEADLIEST SPIDERS

	Spider/scientific name	Range
1	Banana spider (*Phonenutria nigriventer*)	Central and South America
2	Sydney funnel web (*Atrax robustus*)	Australia
3	Wolf spider (*Lycosa raptoria/erythrognatha*)	Central and South America
4	Black widow (*Latrodectus* species)	Widespread
5	Violin spider/Recluse spider (*Loxesceles reclusa*)	Widespread
6	Sac spider (*Cheiracanthium punctorium*)	Central Europe
7	Tarantula (*Eurypelma rubropilosum*)	Neotropics
8	Tarantula (*Acanthoscurria atrox*)	Neotropics
9	Tarantula (*Lasiodora klugi*)	Neotropics
10	Tarantula (*Pamphobeteus* species)	Neotropics

This list ranks spiders according to their "lethal potential"—their venom yield divided by their venom potency. The banana spider, for example, yields 6 mg of venom, with 1 mg the estimated lethal dose in man. However, few spiders are capable of killing humans—there were just 14 recorded deaths caused by black widows in the USA in the entire 19th century—since their venom yield is relatively low compared with that of the most dangerous snakes. The tarantula, for example, produces 1.5 mg of venom, but the lethal dose for an adult human is 12 mg. Anecdotal evidence suggests that the Thailand and Sumatran black bird-eaters may be equally dangerous, but there is insufficient data available.

MAN AND BEAST

FASTEST MAMMALS

	Mammal/scientific name	Maximum recorded speed*
1	Cheetah (*Acinonyx jubatus*)	71 mph (114 km/h)
2	Pronghorn antelope (*Antilocapra americana*)	57 mph (95 km/h)
3=	Blue wildebeest (brindled gnu) (*Connochaetes taurinus*)	50 mph (80 km/h)
=	Lion (*Panthera leo*)	50 mph (80 km/h)
=	Springbok (*Antidorcas marsupialis*)	50 mph (80 km/h)
6=	Brown hare (*Lepus capensis*)	48 mph (77 km/h)
=	Red fox (*Vulpes vulpes*)	48 mph (77 km/h)
8=	Grant's gazelle (*Gazella granti*)	47 mph (76 km/h)
=	Thomson's gazelle (*Gazella thomsonii*)	47 mph (76 km/h)
10	Horse (*Equus caballus*)	45 mph (72 km/h)

*Of those species for which data are available

Along with its relatively slow rivals, the cheetah can deliver its astonishing maximum speed over only fairly short distances. For comparison, the human male 100-meter record (held by Usain Bolt, Jamaica, 2009) stands at 9.58 seconds, equivalent to a speed of 23 mph (37.6 km/h), so all the mammals in the Top 10, and several others, are capable of outrunning a man. If a human ran the 100-meter race at the cheetah's speed, the record would fall to 3 seconds.

SLOWEST MAMMALS

	Mammal/scientific name	Average speed*
1	Three-toed sloth (*Bradypus variegates*)	0.06–0.19 mph (0.1–0.3 km/h)
2	Short-tailed (giant mole) shrew (*Blarina brevicauda*)	1.4 mph (2.2 km/h)
3=	Pine vole (*Microtus pinetorum*)	2.6 mph (4.2 km/h)
=	Red-backed vole (*Clethrionomys gapperi*)	2.6 mph (4.2 km/h)
5	Opossum (order *Didelphimorphia*)	2.7 mph (4.4 km/h)
6	Deer mouse (order *Peromyscus*)	2.8 mph (4.5 km/h)
7	Woodland jumping mouse (*Napaeozapus insignis*)	3.3 mph (5.3 km/h)
8	Meadow jumping mouse (*Zapus hudsonius*)	3.4 mph (5.5 km/h)
9	Meadow mouse or meadow vole (*Microtus pennsylvanicus*)	4.1 mph (6.6 km/h)
10	White-footed mouse (*Peromyscus leucopus*)	4.2 mph (6.8 km/h)

* Of those species for which data are available

SLEEPIEST MAMMALS

Mammal/scientific name	Average hours of sleep per day*
1= Lion (*Panthera leo*)	20
= Three-toed sloth (*Bradypus variegates*)	20
3 Little brown bat (*Myotis lucifugus*)	19.9
4 Big brown bat (*Eptesicus fuscus*)	19.7
5= Opossum (*Didelphis virginiana*)	19.4
= Water opossum (Yapok) (*Chironectes minimus*)	19.4
7 Giant armadillo (*Priodontes maximus*)	18.1
8 Koala (*Phascolarctos cinereus*)	18
9 Nine-banded armadillo (*Dasypus novemcinctus*)	17.4
10 Southern owl monkey (*Aotus azarai*)	17

*Of those species for which data are available

The list excludes periods of hibernation, which can last up to several months among creatures such as the ground squirrel, marmot, and brown bear. At the other end of the scale comes the frantic shrew, which has to hunt and eat constantly or perish.

HEAVIEST DINOSAURS EVER DISCOVERED

Name	Estimated weight

1 *Bruhathkayosaurus* **193–242 tons (175–220 tonnes)**
Fossil remains of this dinosaur were found in southern India. Claims of its gigantic size have been questioned, but some authorities have estimated it may have been up to 145 ft (44 m) long and weighed as much as a blue whale.

2 *Amphicoelias* **134 tons (122 tonnes)**
Its massive size, with a length of some 82 ft (25 m), has been extrapolated from vertebrae fragments discovered in Colorado in 1877, but since lost.

3= *Argentinosaurus* **88–110 tons (80–100 tonnes)**
An Argentinian farmer discovered a 6-ft (1.8-m) long bone in 1988. The dinosaur may have been 72–85 ft (22–26 m) in length.

= *Puertasaurus* **88–110 tons (80–100 tonnes)**
Found in Patagonia, it may have measured as much as 115–131 ft (35–40 m).

5 *Argyrosaurus* **>88 tons (80 tonnes)**
This South American dinosaur, whose name means "silver lizard," was perhaps 66–98 ft (20–30 m) long.

6 *Paralititan* **72–88 tons (65–80 tonnes)**
Remains discovered in the Sahara Desert in Egypt suggest that this was a giant plant-eater, possibly up to 80 ft (24 m) in length. Its humerus (upper arm bone) measures 5 ft 7 in (1.69 m), 14 percent longer than that of any dinosaur previously discovered.

7 *Antarctosaurus* **76 tons (69 tonnes)**
This name, which means "southern lizard," was coined in 1929 by German paleontologist Friedrich von Huene. The creature's thighbone alone measures 7 ft 6 in (2.3 m) and a total length of 60 ft (18 m) has been estimated. Some authorities have put its weight as high as 88 tons (80 tonnes).

8   *Sauroposeidon*   **55–66 tons (50–60 tonnes)**

Known only from vertebrae discovered in Oklahoma in 1994, this may have been the tallest of all dinosaurs at 55 ft 10 in (17 m)

9   *Brachiosaurus*   **53–62 tons (48–56 tonnes)**

This name, which means "arm lizard," was coined in 1903 by US paleontologist Elmer S. Riggs. Some paleontologists have suggested the dinosaur, which was 82 ft (25 m) long, weighed as much as 209 tons (190 tonnes), but this seems improbable (if not impossible, in the light of theories of the maximum possible weight of terrestrial animals).

10   *Supersaurus*   **44–55 tons (40–50 tonnes)**

Fragments of *Supersaurus* were unearthed in Colorado in 1972. It may have measured up to 130 ft (40 m) long. Another specimen, known as "Jimbo," has been discovered in Wyoming and is undergoing examination.

Weights and lengths of dinosaurs have often been estimated from only a few surviving fossilized bones, and there is much dispute even among experts about these. This Top 10 is based on the most reliable recent evidence and indicates the probable ranges, but as more and more information is assembled, these are undergoing constant revision. Some dinosaurs, such as *Diplodocus*, had squat bodies but extended necks, which made them extremely long but not necessarily immensely heavy. Everyone's favorite dinosaur, *Tyrannosaurus rex* ("tyrant lizard"), does not appear in the Top 10 list because although it was one of the fiercest flesh-eating dinosaurs, it was not as large as many of the herbivorous ones. However, measuring a probable 39 ft (12 m) and weighing more than 6.6 tons (6 tonnes), it certainly ranks as one of the largest flesh-eating animals yet discovered. To compare these sizes with living animals, note that the largest recorded crocodile measured 20 ft 4 in (6.2 m) and the largest elephant 35 ft (10.7 m) from trunk to tail and weighed about 13.2 tons (12 tonnes).

LONGEST SNAKES

Snake/scientific name	Maximum length
1 Reticulated (royal) python (*Python reticulates*)	32 ft (10 m)
2 Anaconda (*Eunectes murinus*)	28 ft (8.5 m)
3 Indian python (*Python molurus molurus*)	25 ft (7.6 m)
4 Diamond python (*Morelia spilota spilota*)	21 ft (6.4 m)
5 King cobra (*Ophiophagus hannah*)	19 ft (5.8 m)
6 Boa constrictor (*Boa constrictor*)	16 ft (4.9 m)
7 Bushmaster (*Lachesis muta*)	12 ft (3.7 m)
8 Giant brown snake (*Oxyuranus scutellatus*)	11 ft (3.4 m)
9 Diamondback rattlesnake (*Crotalus atrox*)	9 ft (2.7 m)
10 Indigo or gopher snake (*Drymarchon corais*)	8 ft (2.4 m)

Although the South American anaconda is sometimes claimed to be the longest snake, this has never been authenticated: reports of monsters up to 120 ft (36.5 m) have been published, but without material evidence. Former US President and hunting enthusiast Theodore Roosevelt once offered $5,000 to anyone who could produce the skin or vertebrae of an anaconda of more than 30 ft (9 m), but the prize was never won and it seems that the reticulated or royal python maintains its preeminence. The four largest snakes are all constrictors; the king cobra is the longest venomous snake.

FASTEST FLYING INSECTS

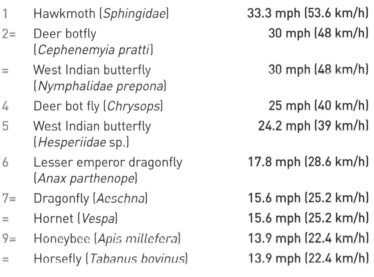

	Insect*/scientific name	Maximum recorded speed
1	Hawkmoth (*Sphingidae*)	33.3 mph (53.6 km/h)
2=	Deer botfly (*Cephenemyia pratti*)	30 mph (48 km/h)
=	West Indian butterfly (*Nymphalidae prepona*)	30 mph (48 km/h)
4	Deer bot fly (*Chrysops*)	25 mph (40 km/h)
5	West Indian butterfly (*Hesperiidae* sp.)	24.2 mph (39 km/h)
6	Lesser emperor dragonfly (*Anax parthenope*)	17.8 mph (28.6 km/h)
7=	Dragonfly (*Aeschna*)	15.6 mph (25.2 km/h)
=	Hornet (*Vespa*)	15.6 mph (25.2 km/h)
9=	Honeybee (*Apis millefera*)	13.9 mph (22.4 km/h)
=	Horsefly (*Tabanus bovinus*)	13.9 mph (22.4 km/h)

*Of those species for which data are available

Few accurate assessments of the flying speeds of insects have been attempted, and this Top 10 represents only the results of the handful of scientific studies widely recognized by entomologists. Some experts have also suggested that the male horsefly (*Hybomitra linei wrighti*) is capable of traveling at 90 mph (145 km/h) when in pursuit of a female, while there are exceptional one-off examples, such as the dragonfly allegedly recorded in 1917 by Dr. Robert J. Tilyard flying at a speed of 61 mph (98 km/h). Many so-called records are clearly flawed, however: for example, in 1927 Charles Townsend estimated the flying speed of the deer bot fly at an unbelievable 818 mph (1,317 km/h). If true, it would have broken the sound barrier!

LARGEST SPIDERS

	Spider	Leg span
1	Huntsman spider (*Heteropoda maxima*)	11.8 in (300 mm)
2	Brazilian salmon pink (*Lasiodora parahybana*)	10.6 in (270 mm)
3	Brazilian giant tawny red (*Grammostola mollicoma*)	10.2 in (260 mm)
4=	Goliath tarantula or bird-eating spider (*Theraphosa blondi*)	10 in (254 mm)
=	Wolf spider (*Cupiennius sallei*)	10 in (254 mm)
6	Purple bloom bird-eating spider (*Xenesthis immanis*)	9.1 in (230 mm)
=	*Xenesthis monstrosa*	9.1 in (230 mm)
8	Hercules baboon (*Hysterocrates Hercules*)	8 in (203 mm)
9	*Hysterocrates* sp.	7 in (178 mm)
10	*Tegenaria parietina*	5.5 in (140 mm)

It should be noted that although these represent the average leg spans of the world's largest spiders, their body size is often considerably smaller: for example, that of the *Lasiodora*, found in Brazil, is around 3.6 in (9.2 cm). Exceptional specimens of the Golden silk orbweaver, *Nephila clavipes*, the largest spider found in North America, may qualify for a place at the bottom of this list.

MAMMALS WITH THE HIGHEST SPERM COUNT

	Mammal	Sperm per ejaculation
1	Pig	60–80,000,000,000
2	Donkey	14,500,000,000
3	Horse	11,000,000,000
4	Bull	5–10,000,000,000
5	Zebu	5,000,000,000
6	Buffalo	3,400,000,000
7	Ram	3,000,000,000
8	Goat	2–3,000,000,000
9	Dog	2,000,000,000
10	Rhesus monkey	1,000,000,000
	Human	*200–500,000,000*

HIGHEST CALORIE-CONSUMING COUNTRIES

	Country	Average daily calorie consumption per capita
1	USA	3,830
2	Luxembourg	3,730
3	Belgium	3,700
4	Greece	3,690
5=	Ireland	3,680
=	Italy	3,680
7	Austria	3,650
8	Israel	3,610
9=	France	3,590
=	Portugal	3,590
	Canada	*3,560*

Source: Food and Agriculture Organization of the United Nations

The daily calorie requirement of the average man is 2,700 and the average woman 2,500. Inactive people need fewer, while those engaged in heavy labor might need to increase, perhaps even double, these figures. Calories that are not consumed as energy turn to fat—which is why calorie counting is one of the key aspects of most diets. The high calorie intake of certain countries reflects the high proportion of starchy foods, such as potatoes, bread, and pasta, in the national diet. In many Western countries, though, the high figures simply reflect overeating—especially since they are averages that include men, women, and children, suggesting that large numbers of people are greatly exceeding them.

LOWEST CALORIE-CONSUMING COUNTRIES

	Country	Average daily calorie consumption per capita
1	Democratic Republic of the Congo	1,500
2	Eritrea	1,530
3	Burundi	1,630
4	Comoros	1,800
5	Ethiopia	1,810
6	Haiti	1,840
7	Angola	1,880
8	Zambia	1,890
9	Central African Republic	1,900
10	Sierra Leone	1,910

Source: Food and Agriculture Organization of the United Nations

While weight watchers of the West guzzle their way through 30 percent more than they need, most countries in Western Europe consuming more than 3,000 calories per head, the daily calorie consumption in 13 of the poorest African nations falls below 2,000, with that of Democratic Republic of the Congo standing at 39 percent (1,500) of the USA figure.

HIGHEST FAT-CONSUMING COUNTRIES

	Country	Average daily fat consumption per capita
1=	Belgium	5.78 oz (164 g)
=	Luxembourg	5.78 oz (164 g)
=	USA	5.78 oz (164 g)
4	France	5.75 oz (163 g)
5	Italy	5.57 oz (158 g)
6	Austria	5.47 oz (155 g)
7	Switzerland	5.36 oz (152 g)
8	Spain	5.29 oz (150 g)
9	Canada	5.22 oz (148 g)
10=	Greece	5.15 oz (146 g)
=	Israel	5.15 oz (146 g)

Source: Food and Agriculture Organization of the United Nations

THE 10
LOWEST FAT-CONSUMING COUNTRIES

	Country	Average daily fat consumption per capita
1	Burundi	0.35 oz (10 g)
2=	Ethiopia	0.67 oz (19 g)
=	Rwanda	0.67 oz (19 g)
4	Democratic Republic of the Congo	0.81 oz (23 g)
5=	Bangladesh	0.95 oz (27 g)
=	Madagascar	0.95 oz (27 g)
7	Malawi	1.02 oz (29 g)
8=	Eritrea	1.09 oz (31 g)
=	Haiti	1.09 oz (31 g)
=	Laos	1.09 oz (31 g)

Source: Food and Agriculture Organization of the United Nations

MOST OBESE COUNTRIES

Country	Percentage of obese adults* Men	Women
1 Tonga	46.6	70.3
2 Samoa	32.9	63
3 Nauru	55.7	60.5
4 Egypt	n/a	46.6
5 Niue	15	46
6 Qatar	34.6	45.3
7 Saudi Arabia	26.4	44
8 Lebanon	36.3	38.3
9 Panama	27.9	36.1
10 Paraguay	22.9	35.7
USA	*31.1*	*33.2*
Canada	*22.9*	*23.2*

*Ranked by percentage of obese women (those with a BMI greater than 30)
Source: International Obesity Task Force (IOTF)

MOST EFFECTIVE KEEP-FIT ACTIVITIES

1   Swimming
2   Cycling
3   Rowing
4   Gymnastics
5   Judo
6   Dancing
7   Soccer
8   Jogging
9   Walking (briskly!)
10   Squash

These sports and activities are recommended by keep-fit experts as the best means of acquiring overall fitness, building stamina and strength, and increasing suppleness.

MOST COMMON CAUSES OF HOME ACCIDENTS IN THE USA

	Product*	Estimated number of injuries[†]
1	Stairs, ramps, landings, floors	2,324,938
2	Beds, mattresses, pillows	560,129
3	Chairs, sofas, sofa beds	476,109
4	Bathroom structures and fixtures	330,102
5	Nonglass doors, panels	321,665
6	Tables	309,252
7	Desks, cabinets, shelves, racks	262,171
8	Cans, other containers	248,126
9	Clothing	245,129
10	Ladders, stools	227,769

*Excluding sport and recreational equipment
†2007
Source: US Consumer Product Safety Commission/NEISS (National Electronic Injury Surveillance System)

MOST COMMON ELEMENTS IN THE HUMAN BODY

	Element	Symbol	Average adult* total
1	Oxygen[†]	O	1,721 oz (48,800 g)
2	Carbon	C	649 oz (18,400 g)
3	Hydrogen[†]	H	282 oz (8,000 g)
4	Nitrogen	N	73 oz (2,080 g)
5	Calcium	Ca	39.5 oz (1,120 g)
6	Phosphorus	P	31 oz (880 g)
7=	Potassium	K	5.6 oz (160 g)
=	Sulfur	S	5.6 oz (160 g)
9	Sodium	Na	4 oz (112 g)
10	Chlorine	Cl	3.4 oz (96 g)

*176-lb (80-kg) male
†Mostly combined as water

These 10 elements account for more than 99 percent of the total, the balance comprising minute quantities of metallic elements, including iron—enough (0.17 oz/ 4.8 g) to make a 6-in (15-cm) nail—as well as zinc, tin, and aluminum.

MOST COMMON PHOBIAS

	Object of phobia	Medical term
1	Open spaces	Agoraphobia, cenophobia, or kenophobia
2	Driving	No medical term; can be a symptom of agoraphobia
3	Vomiting	Emetophobia or emitophobia
4	Confined spaces	Claustrophobia, cleisiophobia, cleithrophobia, or clithrophobia
5	Insects	Entomophobia
6	Illness	Nosemophobia
7	Animals	Zoophobia
8	Flying	Aerophobia or aviatophobia
9	Blushing	Erythrophobia
10	Heights	Acrophobia, altophobia, hypsophobia, or hypsiphobia

Source: National Phobics Society

THE HUMAN BODY

A phobia is a morbid fear that is out of all proportion to the object of the fear. Many people would admit to being uncomfortable about these principal phobias, as well as others, such as snakes (ophiophobia), injections (trypanophobia), or ghosts (phasmophobia), but most do not become obsessive about them or allow such fears to rule their lives. True phobias often arise from some incident in childhood when a person was afraid of some object and developed an irrational fear that persists into adulthood. Perhaps surprisingly, the Top 10 does not remain static as "new" phobias become more common: for example, although outside the Top 10, "technophobia," the fear of modern technology such as computers, is increasingly reported. Nowadays, as well as the valuable work done by phobia organizations, some phobias can be cured by taking special desensitization courses: for example, to conquer one's fear of flying. There are many phobias that are much less common than those that appear in the Top 10. Even if only one person has ever been observed with a specific phobia, psychologists have often given it a name, some more bizarre than others, including:

* beards: pogonophobia
* chins: geniophobia
* eggshells: no medical term
* everything: pantophobia, panophobia, panphobia, or pamphobia
* going to bed: clinophobia
* gravity: barophobia
* hair: chaetophobia
* mirrors: eisoptrophobia
* money: chrometophobia
* number 13: terdekaphobia, tridecaphobia, triakaidekaphobia, or triskaidekaphobia
* opening one's eyes: optophobia
* satellites plunging to Earth: keraunothnetophobia
* slime: blennophobia or myxophobia
* string: linonophobia
* teeth: odontophobia

REASONS FOR VISITS TO A PHYSICIAN IN THE USA

	Reasons for visit	Visits*
1	General medical examination	66,389,000
2	Progress visit, not otherwise specified	51,296,000
3	Cough	26,389,000
4	Postoperative visit	23,355,000
5	Routine prenatal examination	21,718,000
6	Gynecological examination	19,379,000
7	Medication, other and unspecified kinds	19,034,000
8	Stomach and adbomical pains, cramps, and spasms	16,007,000
9	Knee symptoms	14,957,000
10	Well baby examination	13,555,000

*2006
Source: National Ambulatory Medical Care Survey/Center for Disease Control/National Center for Health Statistics

A total of 901,954,000 visits were made in 2006, an increase of 78,412,000 since 2000.

COSMETIC SURGERY PROCEDURES IN THE USA

	Procedure	Number performed*
1	Breast augmentation	355,671
2	Liposuction	341,144
3	Cosmetic eyelid surgery	195,104
4	Nose reshaping	152,434
5	Tummy tuck	147,392
6	Breast reduction (women)	139,926
7	Facelift	132,504
8	Breast lift	115,753
9	Forehead lift	44,437
10	Cosmetic ear surgery	24,798

*2008
Source: American Society for Aesthetic Plastic Surgery

In 2008, 1,766,695 surgical and 8,491,861 nonsurgical procedures were performed in the USA. The latter category included 2,464,123 Botox injections—a remarkable 3,782 percent increase over the 65,157 recorded in 1997. The cost was $7,222,233,062 for surgical and $4,559,075,462 for nonsurgical procedures: a total of $11,781,308,524. The most common procedures for men are liposuction (31,453), followed by nose reshaping (30,174), eyelid surgery (28,678), breast reduction (19,124), and hair transplantation (18,062).

10

PRESERVED BODIES AND BODY PARTS IN THE USA

1   James Allen's skin

Jailed for 20 years for the attempted highway robbery of John Frenno in 1833, Allen wrote his autobiography in jail and prior to his 1837 death arranged for a copy to be bound in his own skin by bookbinder Peter Low. It was given to his victim, Frenno, and later donated to the Boston Athenaeum.

2   George Frederick Cooke's skull

After Irish-born actor Cooke (1756–1812) died in New York, Dr. John W. Francis removed his head for phrenological examination. The skull was bequeathed by his descendants to Thomas Jefferson University, Philadelphia, where it is displayed in the Scott Library; it has been loaned for stage performances of *Hamlet*.

3   Samuel Perry Dinsmoor's body

Eccentric Civil War veteran Dinsmoor (1843–1932) left instructions that his body be permanently on public view in a mausoleum in his Garden of Eden, Lucas, Kansas; the site is on the National Register of Historic Places.

4   Thomas Edison's last breath

It is said that Henry Ford arranged for Charles, the son of inventor Thomas Edison, who died on October 18, 1931, to collect his father's last breath in a test tube. It is now exhibited in the Henry Ford Museum in Dearborn, Michigan, with a question mark on the label.

5   Einstein's brain and eyes

Soon after the death of Albert Einstein, a naturalized American citizen, in 1955, his brain was removed by Thomas Stoltz Harvey and photographed, dissected, and subjected to scientific study. Ophthalmologist Henry Abrams acquired Einstein's eyes—it is said that Michael Jackson inquired about purchasing them, along with the remains of Joseph Merrick, "The Elephant Man," which are preserved in London.

6   D. H. Lawrence's ashes

After the death of the British author in France in 1930, his body was cremated and his ashes taken to his ranch in Taos, New Mexico, now on the National Register of Historic Places. There, it is claimed, they were mixed with concrete to create a memorial shrine.

7 Abraham Lincoln's skull fragments

Shards of Lincoln's skull that were removed in Peterson's Boarding House—across the street from Ford's Theater, where, on April 14, 1865, he was shot by John Wilkes Booth—along with the Derringer bullet that killed him, are held by the National Museum of Health and Medicine, Washington, DC.

8 Major John Wesley Powell's brain

At the Battle of Shiloh in 1862, John Wesley Powell (1834–1902) lost his right arm. It was not preserved, but Powell, who became a distinguished geologist, left his brain to the Smithsonian Institution, Washington, DC.

9 Dan Sickles's leg

The controversial politician Daniel Edgar Sickles (1819–1914), who in 1859 was acquitted of murdering Philip Barton Key (the son of Francis Scott Key, author of "The Star Spangled Banner"), lost his leg at the Battle of Gettysburg in 1863. The bone and a cannonball of the type that shattered it are exhibited at the National Museum of Health and Medicine, Washington, DC.

10 George Washington's hair and false teeth

The Academy of Natural Sciences, Philadelphia, has an album of presidential hair, including that of George Washington, John Adams, and Thomas Jefferson, collected by Philadelphia attorney Peter Arvell Browne. One set of Washington's false teeth was stolen in 1976; another, made of hippopotamus ivory and gold—not wood, as is often claimed—is in the collection of the University of Maryland Dental School, Baltimore.

Among other human relics in the USA, not all survived: the bones of revolutionary Thomas Paine, who died in New York in 1809, were exhumed and taken to England, but were lost—although remains claimed to be his right hand and skull have been produced in recent years. The alleged head of bandit Joaquin Murrieta, shot by California Rangers in 1853, was exhibited in public for the then substantial fee of $1, but was lost in the 1906 San Francisco earthquake. Most bizarre of all, an object claimed to be Emperor Napoleon Bonaparte's penis came up, as it were, at auction in Paris in 1977 and was acquired by eminent US urologist Dr. John Kingsley Lattimer of Englewood, New Jersey. He died in 2007, but the imperial artifact is believed to be retained by his family.

COUNTRIES WITH HIGHEST MALE LIFE EXPECTANCY

	Country	Life expectancy at birth, 2010 (years)
1	Andorra	80.3
2	Singapore	79.5
3	Australia	79.3
4	Japan	78.9
5=	Canada	78.7
=	Israel	78.7
=	Sweden	78.7
8=	Iceland	78.6
=	Jordan	78.6
10	Switzerland	78.1

Source: US Census Bureau, International Data Base

COUNTRIES WITH LOWEST MALE LIFE EXPECTANCY

	Country	Life expectancy at birth, 2010 (years)
1	Angola	37.5
2	Zambia	38.8
3	Liberia	40.9
4	Lesotho	41.4
5	Mozambique	42.1
6	Afghanistan	44.5
7	Nigeria	46.5
8	Zimbabwe	48
9=	Somalia	48.1
=	Swaziland	48.1

Source: US Census Bureau, International Data Base

US STATES WITH HIGHEST MALE LIFE EXPECTANCY

	State	Life expectancy at birth (years)
1	Hawaii	77.1
2=	Minnesota	76.5
=	Utah	76.5
4	Colorado	76.1
5=	California	75.9
=	Idaho	75.9
=	New Hampshire	75.9
=	Washington	75.9
9=	Iowa	75.8
=	Massachusetts	75.8
=	North Dakota	75.8
=	Vermont	75.8

Source: US Census Bureau, *Average Life Expectancy at Birth by State for 2000*

THE 10
US STATES WITH LOWEST MALE LIFE EXPECTANCY

	State	Life expectancy at birth (years)
1	District of Columbia	68.5
2	Mississippi	70.4
3	Louisiana	71.2
4	Alabama	71.3
5	South Carolina	71.6
6	Tennessee	71.8
7	Arkansas	72.1
8=	Georgia	72.3
=	Kentucky	72.3
=	West Virginia	72.3

Source: US Census Bureau, *Average Life Expectancy at Birth by State for 2000*

MOST COMMON CAUSES OF DEATH BY INFECTIOUS AND PARASITIC DISEASES

	Cause	Approximate deaths*
1	Lower respiratory infections	3,884,000
2	HIV/AIDS	2,777,000
3	Diarrheal diseases	1,798,000
4	Tuberculosis	1,566,000
5	Malaria	1,272,000
6	Measles	611,000
7	Whooping cough (pertussis)	294,000
8	Neonatal tetanus	214,000
9	Meningitis	173,000
10	Syphilis	157,000

*For 2002
Source: World Health Organization, *World Health Report 2004*

In 2002, infectious and parasitic diseases accounted for some 10,904,000 of the 57,029,000 deaths worldwide. After declining, certain childhood diseases, including measles and whooping cough, showed an increase.

THE 10
MOST COMMON CAUSES OF DEATH OF MEN IN THE USA

	Cause	Total*
1	Diseases of the heart	315,706
2	Cancer	290,069
3	Accidents (unintentional injuries)	78,941
4	Chronic lower respiratory diseases	59,260
5	Cerebrovascular diseases	54,524
6	Diabetes	36,006
7	Transportation accidents	34,065
8	Intentional self-harm (suicide)	26,308
9	Pneumonia and influenza	25,650
10	Nephritis, nephrotic syndrome, and nephrosis	22,094
	Top 10 total	*942,623*
	Total (all causes)	*1,201,942*

*Latest available data, 2006
Source: National Center for Health Statistics

MOST SUICIDAL US STATES

	State	Suicides*
1	California	3,206
2	Texas	2,418
3	Florida	2,347
4	Pennsylvania	1,430
5	Ohio	1,341
6	New York	1,189
7	Michigan	1,108
8	Illinois	1,086
9	North Carolina	1,009
10	Arizona	945
	Top 10 total	*16,079*
	US total	*32,637*

*Latest available data, 2005
Source: National Center for Health Statistics, 2008

Suicide is the 11th most common cause of death overall among the US population. Male suicides comprise 80 percent of the total, a rate of 18.9 per 100,000 of population, 4.2 times that of female suicides (4.5 per 100,000). Firearms are the leading method, which make up 6.3 percent of the total.

US CELEBRITIES WHO DIED VIOLENTLY

1   **Kurt Cobain**
The 27-year-old member of Nirvana committed suicide with a shotgun on about April 5, 1994 (his body was not discovered until April 8).

2   **Dimebag Darrell**
The guitarist was shot dead on stage at Alrosa Villa, Columbus, Ohio, on December 8, 2004, by Nathan Gale.

3   **James Dean**
The actor was killed on September 20, 1955, in a car crash on US Route 466.

4   **Peg Entwistle**
The British-born starlet jumped off the "H" of the "Hollywood(land)" sign on September 16, 1932.

5   **Marvin Gaye**
The singer was shot in Los Angeles, California, by his father on April 1, 1984.

6   **Brian Harvey**
The musician, his wife, and two children were murdered at their home in Richmond, Virginia, on January 1, 2006.

7   **Donnie Hathaway**
Soul singer Hathaway committed suicide on January 13, 1979, by jumping out of the window of his New York City hotel.

8   **Buddy Holly**
Popular singer Holly was killed when his Beechcraft Bonanza plane crashed near Clear Lake, Iowa, on February 3, 1959.

9   **John Lennon**
British-born US citizen and former Beatle Lennon was shot dead in New York City by Mark Chapman on December 8, 1980.

10 **Margaret Mitchell**
The writer died in Atlanta, Georgia, on August 16, 1949, after being struck by a car driven by Hugh Gravitt, who was convicted of involuntary manslaughter.

FAMOUS PEOPLE WHO DIED WHILE PERFORMING

1 Michael DiBiase

A professional wrestler, Michael DiBiase (1923–69) suffered a heart attack during a match against Man Mountain Mike at Lubbock, Texas, on July 2, 1969. He was buried at Sunset Cemetery, Cochise County, Arizona.

2 Nelson Eddy

Singer and actor Nelson Eddy (1901–67) died of a stroke during a performance at the Sans Souci Hotel, Palm Beach, Florida. He was interred at Hollywood Forever Cemetery, Hollywood, California.

3 Brandon Lee

The son of martial arts actor Bruce Lee, Brandon Lee (1965–93) was accidentally shot on the set of *The Crow*, during filming at Wilmington, North Carolina, on March 31, 1993. He was buried alongside his father at Lake View Cemetery, Seattle, Washington.

4 Vic Morrow

The actor (1929–82) was decapitated and two children were killed when a helicopter went out of control on the set of *Twilight Zone: The Movie*, on July 23, 1982. He was buried at Hillside Memorial Park, Culver City, California.

5 Tyrone Power

The US actor suffered a heart attack while filming a duel scene with George Sanders in *Solomon and Sheba*, in Madrid, Spain, on November 15, 1958. His tomb at Hollywood Forever Cemetery, Hollywood, California, is surmounted by a marble bench.

6 Dick Shawn

When comedian Dick Shawn (1923–87), best known for his role in the movie *The Producers* (1968), collapsed and died on stage at the University of California, San Diego's Mandeville Hall, his audience believed it was part of his routine. He was laid to rest at the Hillside Memorial Park, Culver City, Los Angeles, California.

7   Tiny Tim

Falsetto-voiced singer Tiny Tim (Herbert Khaury, 1932–96) was performing at The Woman's Club of Minneapolis when he suffered a heart attack while singing his best-known song, "Tiptoe Through the Tulips," dying soon afterward. He was interred at Lakewood Cemetery, Minneapolis.

8   Karl Wallenda

The veteran German high-wire performer (1905–78) fell to his death while walking a tightrope between two buildings in San Juan, Puerto Rico, on March 22, 1978. He was buried at Manasota Memorial Park, Bradenton, Florida.

9   Leonard Warren

During a performance of *Simon Boccanegra* at the Metropolitan Opera House, New York, on March 1, 1960, having sung an aria that contains the line "to die, a momentous thing," baritone Warren (1911–60) died of a cerebral hemorrhage. His grave is in Saint Mary's Cemetery, Greenwich, Connecticut.

10   Johnny "Guitar" Watson

American blues guitarist Watson (1935–96) died on stage in Yokohama, Japan, on May 17, 1996. It is claimed his last words were "Ain't that a bitch!" His body was flown back to the USA for burial at Forest Lawn Memorial Park Cemetery, Glendale, California.

On the international stage, there is a long history of actors and musicians dying while performing. French actor-playwright Molière (Jean-Baptiste Poquelin) collapsed on stage in Paris, France, on February 17, 1673, while performing the title role in *Le Malade Imaginaire* (*The Hypochondriac*) and died the following day. Felix Mottl, a celebrated Austrian conductor, died in Munich, Germany, on July 2, 1911, as he conducted his 100th performance of Wagner's *Tristan and Isolde*. William Ellsworth Robinson, an American magician who used the stage name Chung Ling-Soo, was shot at the Wood Green Empire, London, England, on March 23, 1918, while attempting his popular trick of apparently catching bullets in his teeth and died the next day. On May 3, 1972, Les Harvey, singer in British rock band *Stone the Crows*, was electrocuted by his microphone on stage at Swansea, Wales.

SHORTEST-REIGNING POPES

	Pope	In office	Duration (days)
1	Urban VII	Sep 15–27, 1590	12
2=	Boniface VI	Apr 896*	16
=	Celestine IV	Oct 25–Nov 10, 1241	16
4=	Sisinnius	Jan 15–Feb 4, 708	20
=	Theodore II	Dec 897*	20
6=	Damasus II	Jul 17–Aug 9, 1048	23
=	Marcellus II	Apr 9–May 1, 1555	23
8=	Pius III	Sep 22–Oct 18, 1503	26
=	Leo XI	Apr 1–27, 1605	26
10	Benedict V	May 22–Jun 23, 964	32

*Precise dates unknown

A total of 11 popes have reigned for less than 33 days. Some authorities give Pope-elect Stephen's three days (March 23–26, 752) as the shortest reign, but he died before he was consecrated and is therefore not included in the official list of popes (in fact, his successor was given his title, Stephen II, and reigned for five years—although some call his predecessor "Stephen II" and *his* successors are confusingly known as "Stephen II(III)," and so on). Many of those in this list were already elderly and in poor health when they were elected: Boniface VI, Sisinnius, and Pius III were all said to have suffered from severe gout. In addition, the lives of several were far from tranquil: Boniface VI was deposed, and Damasus II possibly poisoned. Pope Johns have been particularly unfortunate: John XXI lasted nine months but was killed in 1277 when a ceiling collapsed on him, while John XII was beaten to death by the husband of a woman with whom he was having an affair. In modern times, John Paul I was pontiff for just 33 days (Aug 26–Sep 28, 1978), his death prompting allegations of poisoning. He was succeeded by John Paul II, whose reign of 26 years, 5 months, and 17 days (Oct 16, 1978–Apr 2, 2005) was the second longest.

US STATES WITH MOST DIVORCES

	State*	Divorces†
1	Florida	82,055
2	Texas	77,649
3	New York	52,251
4	Ohio	39,009
5	North Carolina	35,086
6	Pennsylvania	34,089
7	Michigan	33,812
8	Illinois	32,237
9	Virginia	29,713
10	Tennessee	26,390

*Comparative data for California, Georgia, Hawaii, Indiana, Louisiana, and Minnesota not available
†2008
Source: National Center for Health Statistics, *National Vital Statistics Reports*, Vol. 57, No. 19, July 29, 2009

US STATES WITH THE HIGHEST MARRIAGE RATE

	State	Rate*
1	Alaska	27.8
2	Utah	27.6
3	Wyoming	27.5
4	Idaho	26.6
5	North Dakota	26.3
6	Arkansas	25.6
7	Nebraska	25.3
8	Kansas	24.7
9	Oklahoma	24.4
10	New Mexico	23.0
	US average	*19.6*

*Marriages per 1,000 men aged 15 years and over in the last year
Source: US Census Bureau, *2008 American Community Survey*

MAN AND WIFE

US STATES WITH THE LOWEST MARRIAGE RATE

	State	Rate*
1	Massachusetts	15.1
2	South Carolina	15.7
3=	Delaware	15.8
=	Vermont	15.8
5	Pennsylvania	16.0
6	Rhode Island	16.5
7	Michigan	16.7
8	Maine	16.9
9	New York	17.1
10	Connecticut	17.4

*Marriages per 1,000 men aged 15 years and over in the last year
Source: US Census Bureau, *2008 American Community Survey*

US STATES WHERE WOMEN MARRY THE YOUNGEST

	State	Average age at first marriage
1	Utah	22.8
2	Idaho	23.5
3	Arkansas	24
4	Wyoming	24.1
5	Oklahoma	24.5
6	Kansas	24.7
7	Kentucky	24.8
8	Iowa	25
9=	Alaska	25.2
=	Alabama	25.2
=	Texas	25.2
=	West Virginia	25.2
	US average	*26*
	Oldest: Massachusetts	*28.5*

Source: US Census Bureau, *American Community Survey*

FOREIGN HONEYMOON DESTINATIONS FOR US COUPLES*

1   Italy
2   Hawaii
3   Tahiti
4   France
5   Greece
6   Bali
7   Mexico
8   Fiji
9   Maldives
10   St. Lucia

*Based on a 2009 poll of 6,000 travel agents
Source: *Modern Bride* magazine

REASONS FOR MARITAL BREAKDOWN AND DIVORCE IN THE USA

1   Infidelity
2   Communication breakdown
3   Physical, psychological, or emotional abuse
4   Financial issues
5   Sexual incompatibility
6   Boredom
7   Religious and cultural strains
8   Child-rearing issues
9   Addiction
10 Differences in priorities and expectations

Source: www.divorceguide.com

US INTERNET DATING WEBSITES

	Site	US hits*
1	PlentyofFish	36,825,000
2	Singlesnet	29,896,000
3	eHarmony	19,269,000
4	Match.com	18,329,000
5	Yahoo!Personals	16,365,000
6	People Media sites	12,340,000
7	TRUE.com	10,716,000
8	SparkNetworks	9,124,000
9	Mate1.com	4,847,000
10	OK Cupid	3,714,000

*During a six-month period
Source: ComScore, Inc.

MISS WORLD COUNTRIES*

	Country	Wins	1st runner-up	2nd runner-up	Total points
1	UK†	4	6	4	28
2	Venezuela	5	2	3	22
3	USA	2	5	2	18
4	India	5	1	0	17
5	South Africa	2	2	5	15
6	Australia	2	2	4	14
7	Israel	1	2	6	13
8=	Jamaica	3	0	2	11
=	Sweden	3	1	0	11
10=	Argentina	2	2	0	10
=	Iceland	3	0	1	10
=	France	1	3	1	10

*Based on 3 points for win, 2 for 1st runner-up, 2nd for second runner-up
†Excluding Helen Morgan, who won in 1974, but resigned

MOST COMMON FIRST NAMES OF *PLAYBOY* PLAYMATES

	Name	Appearances
1	Jennifer/Jenny	12
2	Karen/Karin	11
3=	Debbie/Debi/Deborah/Debra	10
=	Susan/Susie/Suzie	10
=	Teri/Terre/Terri/Terry	10
=	Vicki/Victoria	10
7	Kimberly/Kimberley	8
8=	Carol	7
=	Heather	7
=	Nancy	7

A total of 677 *Playboy* Playmates have appeared as the magazine's centerfold, from Marilyn Monroe in December 1954 to Heather Rae Young in December 2009. Several have been featured more than once, and some with another Playmate, including Jennifer and Natalie Jo Campbell (December 2008), *Playboy*'s fifth pair of identical twins.

LAST WOMEN TO TOP MR. BLACKWELL'S "WORST DRESSED" LIST

2007   Victoria "Posh Spice" Beckham

2006   Paris Hilton, Britney Spears (tie)

2005   Britney Spears

2004   Nicollette Sheridan (*Desperate Housewives* actress)

2003   Paris Hilton

2002   Anna Nicole Smith

2001   Anne Robinson (*Weakest Link* host)

2000   Britney Spears

1999   Cher

1998   Linda Tripp (Clinton scandal)

Known as "Mr. Blackwell," waspish US fashion critic Richard Blackwell (1922–2008) became famed for his annual list of "10 Worst Dressed Women," which received widespread media attention during its 48-year span (1960–2007). Previous "winners" included Madonna, Queen Elizabeth, and Zsa Zsa Gabor (twice). Men with a penchant for flamboyant dress have won on two occasions: Howard Stern in 1995 and Dennis Rodman in 1996.

TERMS OF ENDEARMENT IN THE USA

1   Honey

2   Baby

3   Sweetheart

4   Dear

5   Lover

6   Darling

7   Sugar

8=   Angel

=   Pumpkin

10=   Beautiful

=   Precious

A survey conducted on behalf of Korbel Champagne Cellars' Department of Romance, Weddings and Entertaining established that barely 6 percent of the nation used their partner's name but that 26 percent of American adults favored "Honey" as their most frequently used term of endearment, with the rest of the list close runners-up. Curiously, identical numbers were undecided about whether to call their loved one an angel or a pumpkin, while among the more unusual terms were Toots, Snuggles, Huggybear, Little Red, Punky, Tootsie, Buddy, and Pupkins.

LATEST WINNERS OF *MAXIM* MAGAZINE'S "HOT 100" POLL

	Winner	**Runner-up**
2009	Olivia Wilde	Megan Fox
2008	Marisa Miller	Scarlett Johansson
2007	Lindsay Lohan	Jessica Alba
2006	Eva Longoria	Jessica Alba
2005	Eva Longoria	Evangeline Lilly
2004	Jessica Simpson	Beyoncé Knowles
2003	Christina Aguilera	Shania Twain
2002	Jennifer Garner	Kirsten Dunst
2001	Jessica Alba	Kirsten Dunst
2000	Estella Warren	Mena Suvari

MOST SEARCHED-FOR WOMEN ON THE INTERNET*

1   Angelina Jolie
2   Sarah Palin
3   Oprah Winfrey
4   Hillary Clinton
5   Gina Caro
6   Tina Fey
7   Michelle Obama
8   Katie Couric
9   Barbara Walters
10 Dara Torres

*Yahoo! survey, 2008

FIRST NAMES IN THE USA, 1900s*

	Boys		Girls
1	John	1	Mary
2	William	2	Helen
3	James	3	Margaret
4	George	4	Anna
5	Charles	5	Ruth
6	Robert	6	Elizabeth
7	Joseph	7	Dorothy
8	Frank	8	Marie
9	Edward	9	Florence
10	Thomas	10	Mildred

*Based on the most popular names of boys (1,467,664 births) and girls (3,105,534 births) during the decade
Source: Social Security Administration

FIRST NAMES IN THE USA, 1950s*

	Boys			Girls
1	James		1	Mary
2	Michael		2	Linda
3	Robert		3	Patricia
4	John		4	Susan
5	David		5	Deborah
6	William		6	Barbara
7	Richard		7	Debra
8	Thomas		8	Karen
9	Mark		9	Nancy
10	Charles		10	Donna

*Based on the most popular names of boys (20,489,548 births) and girls (19,723,422 births) during the decade
Source: Social Security Administration

FIRST NAMES IN THE USA, 2008

	Boys		Girls
1	Jacob	1	Emma
2	Michael	2	Isabella
3	Ethan	3	Emily
4	Joshua	4	Madison
5	Daniel	5	Ava
6	Alexander	6	Olivia
7	Anthony	7	Sophia
8	William	8	Abigail
9	Christopher	9	Elizabeth
10	Matthew	10	Chloe

Source: Social Security Administration

Jacob has been America's most popular boy's name since 1999. When records began in 1880, it was ranked 39th, and steadily fell out of favor, hitting an all-time low of 367th in 1967, steadily rising to enter the Top 10 in 1993. Michael maintained a consecutive run at #1 from 1961 to 1998. John (20th in 2008) was #1 from 1880 to 1923, while William held the #2 slot from 1880 to 1920 (except for 1910, when it fell to 3rd, behind James).

NAMES TO CONJURE WITH

"CRIMINAL" BOYS' NAMES IN THE USA*

1   Alec

2   Ernest

3   Garland

4   Ivan

5   Kareem

6   Luke

7   Malcolm

8   Preston

9   Tyrell

10   Walter

*Listed alphabetically
Source: *Social Science Quarterly*

Research conducted by Professor David Kalist of Shippensburg University, Pennsylvania, based on a study of more than 15,000 names, appears to indicate that certain names predispose their bearers to lead lives of crime. Whether this results from a bias against certain names, so that those who bear them are subjected to bullying and turn to crime, or other factors, remains unproven.

COUNTRIES WITH THE HIGHEST REPORTED CRIME RATES

	Country	Reported crimes per 100,000 population
1	Dominica	11,382
2	New Zealand	10,588
3	Finland	10,153
4	Denmark	9,283
5	Chile	8,823
6	UK	8,555
7	Montserrat	8,040
8	United States	8,007
9	Netherlands	7,958
10	South Africa	7,719

Source: United Nations

An appearance in this list does not necessarily confirm these as the most crime-ridden countries, since the rate of reporting relates closely to such factors as confidence in local law-enforcement authorities. However, a rate of approximately 1,000 crimes per 100,000 population may be considered average, so those countries in the Top 10 are well above it.

US STATES WITH THE HIGHEST REPORTED CRIME RATES

	State	Reported crimes* Property	Violent
1	Washington, DC	5,104.6	**1,437.7**
2	South Carolina	4,234.2	**729.7**
3	Nevada	3,447.5	**724.5**
4	Tennessee	4,042.6	**722.4**
5	Delaware	3,585.3	**703.4**
6	Florida	4,140.8	**688.9**
7	Louisiana	3,823.1	**656.2**
8	Alaska	2,932.3	**651.9**
9	New Mexico	3,909.2	**649.9**
10	Maryland	3,517.6	**628.2**

*Per 100,000 (2008), ranked by violent crimes per 100,000 population
Source: *FBI Uniform Crime Reports*

These figures should be taken only as a general overview—the FBI itself cautions against ranking, as there are many variables—ranging from the extent of urbanization and cultural factors to the climate of a given state—that have an impact on crime statistics.

MOST COMMON CRIMES IN THE USA

	Crime	Number recorded*
1	Property crime	8,988,919
2	Larceny-theft	5,970,603
3	Burglary	1,989,593
4	Violent crime	1,305,814
5	Motor vehicle theft	1,028,723
6	Aggravated assault	789,254
7	Robbery	422,184
8	Forcible rape	78,669
9	Arson	62,000
10	Murder and nonnegligent manslaughter	15,707
	Total	*20,651,466*

*2007
Source: US Justice Department/FBI, *Crime in the United States 2008*

THE 10
COUNTRIES WITH THE HIGHEST PRISON POPULATIONS

	Country	Prisoners per 100,000 population	Total prisoners*
1	USA	760	2,310,984
2	China	119	1,565,771
3	Russia	622	880,671
4	Brazil	242	469,546
5	India	33	373,271
6	Mexico	208	227,735
7	Thailand	303	199,607
8	South Africa	330	163,479
9	Iran	222	158,351
10	Ukraine	314	144,380
	Canada	*116*	*38,348*

*As of date of most recent data
Source: International Centre for Prison Studies

US STATES WITH MOST PRISON INMATES*

	State	Inmates
1	California	173,320
2	Texas	173,232
3	Florida	100,494
4	New York	62,211
5	Georgia	54,016
6	Ohio	51,160
7	Michigan	50,482
8	Pennsylvania	46,313
9	Illinois	45,675
10	Virginia	39,224

*State and Federal prisoners, as of June 30, 2008
Source: Department of Justice

CELEBRITIES JAILED IN THE USA

	Name	Crime	Sentenced
1	Chuck Berry, musician	Armed robbery	1944
2	Zsa Zsa Gabor, actress	Assault of a police officer	1989
3	Paris Hilton, socialite	Violation of a probation order	2007
4	Tommy Lee, musician	Spousal abuse	1998
5	Bernie Madoff, trader	Investment fraud	2009
6	O.J. Simpson, football player	Armed robbery	2008
7	Phil Spector, music producer	Second degree murder	2009
8	Martha Stewart, writer, TV presenter	Stock trading violations	2005
9	Mike Tyson, boxer	Rape	1992
10	Mark Wahlberg, actor	Assault	1987

THE 10

CRIMINALS LONGEST ON THE FBI'S "10 MOST WANTED" LIST

	Fugitive (FBI no.)	Crime
1	Donald Eugene Webb (375)	Alleged cop killer
2	Victor Manuel Gerena (386)	Armed robbery
3	Charles Lee Heron (265)	Murder
4	Frederick J. Tenuto (14)	Murder
5	Katherine Ann Power (315)	Bank robbery
6	Glen Stewart Godwin (447)	Murder
7	Arthur Lee Washington Jr. (427)	Attempted murder
8	Osama Bin Laden (456)	Terrorism, murder
9	David Daniel Keegan (78)	Murder, robbery
10	James Eddie Diggs (36)	Alleged murder

Added to list	Removed from list	Period on list		
		Years	**Months**	**Days**
May 4, 1981	Mar 31, 2007	25	10	27
May 14, 1984	*	25	2	18
Feb 9, 1968	Jun 18, 1986	18	4	9
May 24, 1950	Mar 9, 1964	13	9	14
Oct 17, 1970	Jun 15, 1984	13	7	29
Dec 7, 1996	*	12	7	25
Oct 18, 1989	Dec 27, 2000	11	2	19
Jun 7, 1999	*	10	1	25
Jun 21, 1954	Dec 13, 1963	9	5	22
Aug 27, 1952	Dec 14, 1961	9	3	17

*Still at large; periods as of November 25, 2009
Source: FBI

The FBI officially launched its celebrated "10 Most Wanted" list on March 14, 1950. Since then almost 500 criminals have figured on it. Names appear until individuals are captured, die, or charges are dropped. On January 8, 1969, bank robber and double cop murderer Billie Austin Bryant appeared on the list for the record shortest time—just two hours—before he was arrested.

FIRST EXECUTIONS BY ELECTROCUTION IN THE USA

	Name	Age	Prison*	Date
1	William Kemmler	30	Auburn	Aug 6, 1890
2	Harris A. Smiler	32	Sing Sing	Jul 7, 1891
3	James J. Slocum	22	Sing Sing	Jul 7, 1891
4	Joseph Wood	21	Sing Sing	Jul 7, 1891
5	Schihiok Jugigo	35	Sing Sing	Jul 7, 1891
6	Martin D. Loppy	51	Sing Sing	Dec 7, 1891
7	Charles McElvaine	20	Sing Sing	Feb 8, 1892
8	Jeremiah Cotto	40	Sing Sing	Mar 28, 1892
9	Joseph L. Tice	63	Auburn	Jun 18, 1892
10	Joseph Wood	37	Clinton	Aug 2, 1892

*All these prisons are located in New York State

The electric chair was installed in Sing Sing Prison, Ossining, New York, in 1891, just a year after it was first used to execute William Kemmler at Auburn Prison, also in New York State. By the end of the 19th century, 29 inmates had been executed by this means. Among the first 10 is the coincidence of two people called Joseph Wood, the first black, the second white. By 1963, when the chair was used for the last time, a total of 614 inmates had been electrocuted at Sing Sing (now called Ossining Correctional Facility). Electrocution is no longer used in New York, but remains either the only or an alternative method of execution in nine states.

FIRST EXECUTIONS BY GAS CHAMBER IN THE USA

	Name	Age	Prison/location	Date
1	Gee Jon	29	Nevada State Prison, Carson City	Feb 8, 1924
2	Stanko Jukich	29	Nevada	May 21, 1926
3	Robert H. White	41	Nevada	Jun 2, 1930
4	Luis Ceja	28	Nevada	Sep 4, 1931
5	John Hall	52	Nevada	Nov 28, 1932
6	Ray Elmer Miller	34	Nevada	May 8, 1933
7	William Kelly	30	Colorado State Penitentiary, Canon City	Jun 22, 1934
8=	Fred Hernandez	19	Arizona State Prison, Florence	Jul 6, 1934
=	Manuel Hernandez	18	Arizona	Jul 6, 1934
10=	George Shaughnessy	19	Arizona	Jul 13, 1934
=	Joseph Behiter	56	Nevada	Jul 13, 1934

THE 10

FIRST EXECUTIONS BY LETHAL INJECTION IN THE USA

	Name	Age	Prison/location	Date
1	Charles Brooks	40	Huntsville, Texas	Dec 7, 1982
2	James Autry	29	Texas	Mar 14, 1984
3	James W. Hutchins	54	Raleigh, North Carolina	Mar 16, 1984
4	Ronald O'Bryan	39	Texas	Mar 31, 1984
5	Thomas Barefoot	39	Texas	Oct 30, 1984
6	Velma Barfield	52	North Carolina	Nov 2, 1984
7	Doyle Skillern	48	Texas	Jan 16, 1985
8	Stephen Morin	37	Texas	Mar 13, 1985
9	Jesse de la Rosa	24	Texas	May 15, 1985
10	Charles Milton	34	Texas	Jun 25, 1985

Execution by lethal injection was first proposed in the late 1880s, but electrocution was introduced in preference. Oklahoma was the first US state to legalize the method, although the option was not taken there until 1990, and most of the first 10 were executed in Texas. Velma Barfield, the first woman to be executed by this method, was also the first woman to be executed in the USA for 22 years. It is now the most commonly used form of execution in the USA. In 1997, China became the first country outside the US to carry out an execution by lethal injection, in "execution vans." In 2009 China announced that this method would replace the more common use of a bullet—for which the victim's family was charged.

THE 10
US STATES WITH MOST PRISONERS ON DEATH ROW

	State	Prisoners under death sentence*
1	California	678
2	Florida	402
3	Texas	358
4	Pennsylvania	226
5	Alabama	207
6	Ohio	181
7	North Carolina	167
8	Arizona	129
9	Georgia	109
10	Tennessee	92

*As of January 1, 2009
Source: Death Penalty Information Center/NAACP Legal Defense and Educational Fund, Inc.

On January 1, 2009, a total of 3,297 prisoners were on death row in 36 states, plus those under US government (55) and US military (9) jurisdiction. The total for individual states is higher (3,306), as some inmates were sentenced in more than one state, and are thus counted more than once. New Mexico abolished the death penalty in March 2009, but two prisoners remain on the state's death row. The highest number of prisoners on death row occurred in 2000, with 3,593 under sentence of death—in marked contrast to the 20th-century low of just 134 in 1973.

MOST STOLEN CARS IN THE USA

1   1994 Honda Accord
2   1995 Honda Civic
3   1989 Toyota Camry
4   1997 Ford F-150 Pickup
5   2004 Dodge Ram Pickup
6   2000 Dodge Caravan
7   1996 Jeep Cherokee/Grand Cherokee
8   1994 Acura Integra
9   1999 Ford Taurus
10 2002 Ford Explorer

Source: National Insurance Crime Bureau, *Hot Wheels 2009*

COUNTRIES WITH THE HIGHEST MURDER RATES

	Country	Murders per 100,000 population*
1	Honduras	58
2	Sierra Leone	50
3	Jamaica	49
4=	El Salvador	48
=	Venezuela	48
6	Guatemala	47
7	Trinidad and Tobago	42
8	Angola	40
9	South Africa	39
10	Colombia	36
	USA	*5.8*

*In latest year for which figures are available

THE 10
WORST GUN MASSACRES IN THE USA*

	Perpetrator	Location	Date	Killed
1	Seung-Hui Cho	Virginia Tech, Blacksburg, Virginia	Apr 16, 2007	**32**

South Korean-born Cho used handguns to kill 27 fellow students and five faculty members at Virginia Tech before turning a gun on himself in America's worst shooting.

	Perpetrator	Location	Date	Killed
2=	James Oliver Huberty	San Ysidro, California	Jul 18, 1984	**22**

Huberty, aged 41, opened fire in a McDonald's restaurant, killing 21 before being shot dead by a SWAT marksman. A further 19 were wounded, including a victim who died the following day.

	Perpetrator	Location	Date	Killed
=	George Jo Hennard	Killeen, Texas	Oct 16, 1991	**22**

Hennard drove his pickup truck through the window of Luby's Cafeteria and, in 11 minutes, killed 22 with semiautomatic pistols before shooting himself.

	Perpetrator	Location	Date	Killed
4	Ronald Gene Simmons	Russellville, Arkansas	Dec 28, 1987	**16**

Simmons, aged 47, killed 16, including 14 members of his own family, by shooting or strangling. He was caught and executed on June 25, 1990.

	Perpetrator	Location	Date	Killed
5	Charles Joseph Whitman	Austin, Texas	Jul 31–Aug 1, 1966	**15**

An ex-Marine marksman, 25-year-old Whitman killed his mother and wife, and the following day took the elevator to the 27th floor of the campus tower and ascended to the observation deck at the University of Texas at Austin, from where he killed 14 and wounded 34 (one of whom died a week later), before being shot dead by police officer Romero Martinez.

| 6 | Patrick Henry Sherrill | Edmond, Oklahoma | Aug 20, 1986 | **14** |

Sherrill, aged 44, shot 14 dead and wounded six others at the post office where he worked before killing himself.

| 7= | Howard Unruh | Camden, New Jersey | Sep 6, 1949 | **13** |

Ex-GI Unruh, aged 28, used a German Luger pistol to kill 13 people at random within 12 minutes. He was captured after a police siege at his house, declared insane, and has remained in mental institutions ever since.

| = | George Banks | Wilkes-Barre and Jenkins Township, Pennsylvania | Sep 25, 1982 | **13** |

State prison guard Banks shot and killed 13, including five of his own children. He was caught and sentenced to death, but has remained in prison ever since.

| = | Willie Mak and Benjamin Ng | Seattle, Washington | Feb 19, 1983 | **13** |

During an armed robbery of Wah Mee, a Chinese gambling club, Mak and Ng shot 13 dead. Mak was sentenced to death, Ng to life imprisonment.

| = | Eric Harris and Dylan Klebold | Columbine High School, Colorado | Apr 20, 1999 | **13** |

Both students at the school, Harris (18) and Klebold (17) went on a gun rampage, killing 12 students and a teacher before committing suicide.

*By individuals, excluding terrorist and military actions; totals exclude perpetrator

MOST PROLIFIC MURDERESSES

Murderess	Victims

1 Countess Erzsébet Báthory   **up to 650**

In the period up to 1610 in Hungary, Báthory (1560–1614), known as "Countess Dracula"—the title of a 1970 Hammer horror movie about her life and crimes—was alleged to have murdered between 300 and 650 girls (her personal list of 610 victims was described at her trial) in the belief that drinking their blood would prevent her from aging. She was eventually arrested in 1611. Tried and found guilty, she died on August 21, 1614, walled up in her own castle at Čachtice (Csejte).

2 Susannah Olah   **up to 100**

At the age of 40, Susi Olah, a nurse and midwife, arrived at Nagzrev, a Hungarian village. Over the next few years she "predicted" the demise of anything up to 100 people who subsequently met their deaths as a result of arsenic poisoning. Many inhabitants believed the woman who came to be nicknamed the "Angel-maker" had prophetic powers, but her victims ranged from newborn and handicapped children to elderly people and the husbands of many of the local women—in most cases with the full complicity of their relatives, and in some instances with their help. When the law finally caught up with her in 1929, she committed suicide.

3 Delfina and Maria de Jesús Gonzales   **91**

In 1964 the Gonzales sisters were sentenced to 40 years' imprisonment after the remains of 80 women and 11 men were discovered on their Mexican property.

4 Bella Poulsdatter Sorensen Gunness   **42**

Bella, or Belle Gunness (1859–1908?), a Norwegian-born immigrant to the US, is believed to have murdered her husband, Peter Gunness, for his life insurance (she claimed that an ax had fallen from a shelf and onto his head). After this, she lured between 16 and 28 suitors through "lonely hearts" advertisements, as well as numerous others—perhaps as many as 42—to her Laporte, Indiana, farm, where she murdered them. On April 28, 1908, her farm was burned down and a headless corpse found there was declared to be Gunness, killed—along with her three children—by her accomplice Ray Lamphere. It is believed that she faked her own death and disappeared.

5   Gesina Margaretha Gottfried   at least 30

Having poisoned her first husband and two children with arsenic in 1815, German murderess Gesina Mittenberg killed both her parents by the same method and then her next husband, whom she married on his deathbed, thereby inheriting his fortune. As her income dwindled, she carried out an extensive series of murders, including those of her brother, a creditor, and most of the family of a Bremen wheelwright called Rumf, for whom she worked as a housekeeper. Rumf himself became suspicious and in 1828 Gottfried was arrested. After a trial at which she admitted to more than 30 murders, she was executed.

6   Jane Toppan   30

Boston-born Nora Kelley, also known as Jane Toppan (1854–1938), worked as a nurse. After numerous patients in her care had died, bodies were exhumed that revealed traces of morphine and atropine poisoning. It seems probable, according to both evidence and her own confession, that she killed as many as 30 victims. She died on August 17, 1938, in an asylum at the age of 84.

7   Hélène Jegado   23

Jegado was a French housemaid who was believed to have committed some 23 murders by arsenic poisoning. She was tried at Rennes in 1851, found guilty, and guillotined in 1852.

8   Genene Jones   21

In 1984 Jones was found guilty of killing a baby, Chelsea McClellan, at the San Antonio, Texas, hospital at which she worked as a nurse, by administering the drug succinylcholine. She was sentenced to 99 years in prison. Jones had been dismissed from the previous hospital at which she had worked after up to 20 babies in her care had died of suspicious but uncertain causes, and some authorities linked her with as many as 42 deaths.

9   Mary Ann Cotton   20

Cotton (b.1832), a former nurse, is generally held to be Britain's worst mass murderess. It seems probable that over a 20-year period she disposed of 14–20 victims, including three husbands, children, and stepchildren, by arsenic poisoning. She was hanged at Durham Prison on March 24, 1873.

10   Waltraud Wagner   15

Wagner was the ringleader but only one of four nurses found guilty of causing numerous deaths through deliberate drug overdoses and other means at the Lainz hospital, Vienna, in the late 1980s. Between 42 and possibly as many as several hundred patients became the victims of the Wagner "death squad," for which she was sentenced to life imprisonment on charges that included 15 counts of murder and 17 of attempted murder.

MOST PROLIFIC SERIAL KILLERS IN THE USA

Murderer	**Victims***

1 Henry Lee Lucas   **200**

Lucas (1936–2001) admitted in 1983 to 360 murders, many committed with his partner-in-crime Ottis Toole. He died while on Death Row in Huntsville Prison, Texas. Some authorities have claimed a tally as high as 600 for America's worst serial killer.

2 Herman Webster Mudgett   **150**

Also known as "H. H. [Henry Howard] Holmes," Mudgett (1860–96), a former doctor, was believed to have lured over 150 women to his 63rd Street, Chicago, "castle," which he operated as a hotel, and which was a warren of secret passages with windowless and soundproofed cells with gas valves. It was fully equipped for torturing, murdering, and dissecting his victims and disposing of their bodies in furnaces or an acid bath. Arrested in 1894 and found guilty of the murder of an ex-partner in crime, Benjamin F. Pitezel, he confessed to killing 27, but may have killed on up to 150 occasions (although there is some evidence that the remains of more than 200 victims were found at his home). Mudgett, regarded as America's first mass murderer, was hanged at Moyamensing Prison, Philadelphia, on May 7, 1896.

3 Donald Henry "Pee Wee" Gaskins   **100–110**

Gaskins (1933–91), of South Carolina, committed his first murder while in prison, from which he escaped but was recaptured. On his release, he began killing hitchhikers. He was arrested in 1976 and charged with eight murders and received a death sentence that was commuted to life imprisonment. While serving his term he killed another inmate, for which he was sentenced to death and electrocuted on September 6, 1991.

4 Randy Steven Kraft   **67**

From 1972 until his arrest on May 14, 1983, Kraft (b.1945) is thought to have murdered up to 67 men. On November 29, 1989, he was found guilty on 16 counts, was sentenced to death, and is currently on death row at San Quentin State Prison, California.

5   Gary Leon Ridgway   48–90

Ridgway (b.1949) became known as the "Green River Killer," for the area in Washington where he preyed on women, killing up to 90 before he was apprehended in 2001. He is serving life in Washington State Penitentiary, Walla Walla, Washington.

6   Gerald Stano   41

Gerald Eugene Stano (1951–98) killed 41 women prior to his arrest in 1980. He was electrocuted at Florida State Prison on March 23, 1998.

7   Richard "The Iceman" Kuklinski   40

Contract killer Kuklinski (1935–2006) may have murdered as many as the 200 he claimed to have killed. He died while in custody in Trenton, New Jersey.

8   Donald Harvey   37–87

Working as an orderly in hospitals in Kentucky and Ohio, Harvey is believed to have murdered some 58 patients up to the time of his arrest in March 1987. He pleaded guilty to 24 murders, for which he received multiple life sentences, later confessing to further charges and receiving additional sentences.

9   Ted Bundy   35–100

Theodore Robert "Ted" Bundy (1946–89) confessed to 30 murders, but is believed to have committed anything up to 100. He was tried in 1979 and sentenced to death, which was carried out in the electric chair at Florida State Prison, Starke, on January 24, 1989.

10 Michael Swango   30–60

Swango (b. 1954) was a doctor who poisoned patients and coworkers with arsenic and other substances in hospitals in the USA. When suspicions were aroused, he moved to Zimbabwe, where he continued to murder patients, but was arrested on a flight to the USA, was tried, and is serving life imprisonment.

*Ranked by minimum estimate; includes only individual murderers; excludes murders by bandits, terrorist groups, and political and military atrocities

Serial killers are mass murderers who kill repeatedly, often over long periods, in contrast to the so-called spree killers who have been responsible for single-occasion massacres. Because of the secrecy surrounding their crimes, and the time spans involved, it is impossible to calculate the precise numbers of their victims. The numbers of murders attributed to the criminals listed should therefore be taken as "best estimates" based on the most reliable evidence available. Such is the magnitude of the crimes of some of these killers, however, that these figures may be underestimates.

MOST COMMON MURDER WEAPONS AND METHODS IN THE USA

	Weapon/method	Victims*
1	Firearms	9,484
2	Knives or cutting instruments	1,897
3	"Personal weapons" (hands, feet, fists, etc.)	861
4	Blunt objects (hammers, clubs, etc.)	614
5	Asphyxiation	89
6	Strangulation	88
7	Fire	86
8	Narcotics	33
9	Drowning	15
10	Explosives	10
=	Poison	10
	Other/weapons not stated	*99*
	Total	*14,180*

*2008
Source: *FBI Uniform Crime Reports*

The order of the weapons used in US murders has changed little in recent years. Perhaps most surprisingly, the proportion of killings involving firearms has gone down compared with the figures for the early years of the 20th century: in 1920, for example, 4,178 out of a total of 5,815 murders were committed with firearms and explosives (then a combined statistic), a total of 72 percent, while in 2008, out of the total cases of murder, 68 percent were committed using firearms. If the relative populations (1920: 106,021,537; 2008: 303,824,640) are taken into account, the overall murder rate has gone down from one in 18,232 to one in 21,426.

LARGEST ARMED FORCES

Estimated active forces

	Country	Army	Navy	Air	Total
1	China	1,600,000	255,000	330,000	**2,185,000**
2	USA	632,245	339,453	340,530	**1,539,587***
3	India	1,100,000	55,000	120,000	**1,281,200†**
4	North Korea	950,000	46,000	110,000	**1,106,000**
5	Russia	360,000	142,000	160,000	**1,027,000‡**
6	South Korea	560,000	68,000	64,000	**692,000**
7	Pakistan	550,000	22,000	45,000	**617,000**
8	Iran	350,000	18,000	30,000	**523,000#**
9	Turkey	402,000	48,600	60,000	**510,600**
10	Egypt	340,000	18,500	30,000	**468,500§**
	Canada	*33,711*	*10,960*	*19,699*	***64,370*****

*Includes 186,661 Marine Corps and 40,698 Coast Guard
†Includes 6,200 Coast Guard
‡Includes 35,000 Airbone Army, 80,000 Strategic Deterrent Forces, and 250,000 Command and Support
#Includes 125,000 Islamic Revolutionary Guard Corps
§Includes 80,000 Air Defense Command
**Includes 2,344 reserves
Source: The International Institute for Strategic Studies, *The Military Balance 2009*

Several countries also have substantial reserves on standby: South Korea's reserve has been estimated at some 4.7 million plus 3.5 paramilitary, Vietnam's at 5 million, and China's at 800,000. North Korea has the highest number of troops in relation to its population: 47.11 per 1,000.

LARGEST ARMED FORCES OF WORLD WAR I

	Country	Personnel*
1	Russia	12,000,000
2	Germany	11,000,000
3	British Empire	8,904,467
4	France	8,410,000
5	Austria-Hungary	7,800,000
6	Italy	5,615,000
7	USA	4,355,000
8	Turkey	2,850,000
9	Bulgaria	1,200,000
10	Japan	800,000

*Total at peak strength

Russia's armed forces were relatively small in relation to the country's population—some 6 percent, compared with 17 percent in Germany. Several other European nations had forces that were similarly substantial in relation to their populations: Serbia's army was equivalent to 14 percent of its population. In total, more than 65 million combatants were involved in fighting some of the costliest battles, in terms of numbers killed, that the world has ever known.

THE 10
COUNTRIES SUFFERING THE GREATEST MILITARY LOSSES IN WORLD WAR I

	Country	Killed
1	Germany	1,773,700
2	Russia	1,700,000
3	France	1,357,800
4	Austria-Hungary	1,200,000
5	British Empire*	908,371
6	Italy	650,000
7	Romania	335,706
8	Turkey	325,000
9	USA	116,516
10	Bulgaria	87,500

*Including Australia, Canada, India, New Zealand, South Africa, etc.

The number of battle fatalities and deaths from other causes among military personnel varied enormously from country to country. Romania's death rate was highest, at 45 percent of its total mobilized forces; Germany's was 16 percent; Austria-Hungary's and Russia's 15 percent; and the British Empire's 10 percent; with the USA's 2 percent and Japan's 0.04 percent among the lowest. Japan's forces totaled only 800,000, of which an estimated 300 were killed, 907 wounded, and just three taken prisoner or reported missing. In contrast, Belgium had 267,000 in the field, with 13,716 killed, 44,686 wounded, and 34,659 prisoners or missing in action.

MEDAL OF HONOR CAMPAIGNS

	Campaign	Years	Medals awarded
1	Civil War	1861–5	1,522
2	World War II	1941–5	464
3	Indian Wars	1861–98	426
4	Vietnam War	1965–73	246
5	Korean War	1950–53	131
6	World War I	1917–18	124
7	Spanish-American War	1898	110
8	Philippine-American War	1899–1913	80
9	Boxer Rebellion	1900	59
10	Mexican Campaign	1914	56

Source: The United States Army

The Congressional Medal of Honor, the USA's highest military award, was first issued in 1863. In addition to the medal itself, recipients receive such benefits as a pension of $1,027 for life, free air travel, and the right to be buried in the Arlington National Cemetery. To date (September 8, 2009), there have been 3,447 recipients, including 19 double recipients, of whom 95 are alive. The most recent recipient was Sergeant First Class Jared C. Monti, posthumously, for service in Afghanistan. His family received the award from President Obama at the White House on September 17, 2009.

US AIR ACES OF WORLD WAR I

	Pilot*	Kills claimed
1	Captain Edward Vernon Rickenbacker	26
2	Captain William C. Lambert	22
3=	Captain August T. Iaccaci	18
=	Second Lieutenant Frank Luke Jr.	18
5=	Captain Frederick W. Gillet	17
=	Major Gervais Raoul Lufbery	17
7=	Captain Howard A. Kuhlberg	16
=	Captain Oren J. Rose	16
9	Captain Clive W. Warman	15
10=	First Lieutenant David Endicott Putnam	13
=	First Lieutenant George Augustus Vaughan Jr.	13

*Includes US pilots flying with RAF and French flying service

The term "ace" was first used during World War I for a pilot who had brought down at least five enemy aircraft. The first-ever reference in print to an air "ace" appeared in an article in the London *Times* (September 14, 1917), which described Raoul Lufbery as "the 'ace' of the American Lafayette Flying Squadron." The names of French pilots who achieved this feat were recorded in official communiqués, but although US and other pilots followed the same system, the definition of an "ace" varied from three to 10 aircraft and was never officially approved, remaining an informal concept during both world wars. The German equivalent was *Oberkanone*, which means "top gun."

GERMAN AIR ACES OF WORLD WAR I

	Pilot	Kills claimed
1	Rittmeister Manfred von Richthofen	80
2	Oberleutnant Ernst Udet	62
3	Oberleutnant Erich Loewenhardt	53
4	Leutnant Werner Voss	48
5=	Hauptmann Bruno Loerzer	45
=	Leutnant Fritz Rumey	45
7	Hauptmann Rudolph Berthold	44
8	Leutnant Paul Bäumer	43
9	Leutnant Josef Jacobs	41
10=	Hauptmann Oswald Boelcke	40
=	Leutnant Franz Büchner	40
=	Oberleutnant Lothar Freiherr von Richthofen	40

The claims of top World War I ace Rittmeister Manfred, Baron von Richthofen (whose brother also merits a place in this list), of 80 kills has been disputed, since only 60 of them have been completely confirmed. Richthofen, known as the "Red Baron" and leader of the so-called Flying Circus (because the aircraft of his squadron were painted in distinctive bright colors), shot down 21 Allied fighters in the single month of April 1917. His own end a year later, on April 21, 1918, has been the subject of controversy ever since, and it remains uncertain whether his Fokker triplane was shot down in aerial combat with British pilot Captain A. Roy Brown (who was credited with the kill), or by shots from Australian machine gunners on the ground. Hermann Goering, commander-in-chief of the Luftwaffe in World War II, was a fighter pilot in Richthofen's Flying Circus, and was the last commander of the squadron before the Armistice of November 11, 1918. He shot down 22 Allied aircraft and was awarded Germany's highest decoration, the Ordre Pour le Mérite, on June 2, 1918. He committed suicide at Nuremberg on October 15, 1946.

LARGEST ARMED FORCES OF WORLD WAR II

	Country	Personnel*
1	USSR	12,500,000
2	USA	12,364,000
3	Germany	10,000,000
4	Japan	6,095,000
5	France	5,700,000
6	UK	4,683,000
7	Italy	4,500,000
8	China	3,800,000
9	India	2,150,000
10	Poland	1,000,000

*Total at peak strength

Allowing for deaths and casualties, the total forces mobilized during the course of the war is, of course, greater than the peak strength figures: that of the USSR, for example, has been put as high as 20 million; the USA 16,354,000; Germany 17.9 million; Japan 9.1 million; and the UK 5,896,000.

US AIR ACES OF WORLD WAR II

	Pilot	Kills claimed
1	Major Richard I. Bong	40
2	Major Thomas B. McGuire	38
3	Commander David S. McCampbell	34
4=	Lieutenant Colonel Gregory Boyington	28
	Colonel Francis S. Gabreski*	28
6=	Major Robert S. Johnson	27
=	Colonel Charles H. MacDonald	27
8	Major Joseph J. Foss	26
9=	Lieutenant Robert M. Hanson	25
=	Major George E. Preddy	25

*Also 6.5 kills in the Korean War

GERMAN AIR ACES OF WORLD WAR II

	Pilot	Kills claimed
1	Major Eric Hartmann	352
2	Major Gerhard Barkhorn	301
3	Major Günther Rall	275
4	Oberst Otto Kittel	267
5	Major Walther Nowotny	258
6	Major Wilhelm Batz	237
7	Major Erich Rudorffer	222
8	Oberst Heinz Bär	220
9	Oberst Hermann Graf	212
10	Major Heinrich Ehrler	209

Although these apparently high claims have been dismissed by some military historians as inflated for propaganda purposes, it is worth noting that many of them relate to kills on the Eastern Front, where the Luftwaffe was undoubtedly superior to its Soviet opponents, and some of them relate to "kills" on the ground. Few have questioned the so-called Blond Knight Eric Hartmann's achievement, however, and his victories over Soviet aircraft so outraged the USSR that after the war he was arrested and sentenced to 25 years in a Russian labor camp. He was released in 1955, returned to serve in the West German air force, and died on September 20, 1993. All those in the Top 10 were day-fighter aces; the highest "score" by a night-fighter pilot was the 121 kills credited to Major Heinz-Wolfgang Schnauffer. A total of 25 pilots achieved more than 150 kills yet failed to make the Top 10.

WARS WITH MOST US MILITARY CASUALTIES

	War	Estimated number killed*
1	Civil War (1861–65)	438,332
2	World War II (1941–45)	405,399
3	World War I (1917–18)	116,516
4	Vietnam War (1965–73)	58,209
5	Korean War (1950–53)	36,574
6	Mexican War (1846–48)	13,283
7	Revolutionary War (1775–83)	10,623
8	Iraq War (2003–)	4,257[†]
9	Philippine-American War (1899–1913)	4,196
10	Spanish-American War (1898)	2,446

*Battle and other deaths
†As of September 2008
Source: United States Department of Veteran Affairs

THE 10
CITIES MOST BOMBED
BY THE USAF AND
RAF, 1939–45

	City	Estimated civilian fatalities
1	Dresden	100,000+
2	Hamburg	55,000
3	Berlin	49,000
4	Cologne	20,000
5	Magdeburg	15,000
6	Kassel	13,000
7	Darmstadt	12,300
8=	Essen	7,500
=	Heilbronn	7,500
10=	Dortmund	6,000
=	Wuppertal	6,000

The high level of casualties in Dresden resulted principally from the saturation bombing and the firestorm that ensued after Allied raids on the lightly defended city. Although their main objective was to destroy the railway marshaling yards, the scale of the raids was massive: 775 British bombers took part in the first night's raid on February 13, 1945, followed the next day by 450 US bombers, with a final attack by 200 US bombers on February 15, while the city was still blazing, with 11 sq miles (28.5 sq km) already devastated by the firestorm. A total of 39,773 were "officially identified dead," but many thousands more were incinerated in buildings and never identified.

COUNTRIES SUFFERING THE GREATEST MILITARY LOSSES IN WORLD WAR II

	Country	Killed
1	USSR	13,600,000*
2	Germany	3,300,000
3	China	1,324,516
4	Japan	1,140,429
5	USA[†]	405,399
6	British Empire[‡] (UK 264,000)	357,116
7	Romania	350,000
8	Poland	320,000
9	Yugoslavia	305,000
10	Italy	279,800
	Total	*21,382,260*

*Total, of which 7.8 million battlefield deaths
†Total, of which 291,557 battlefield deaths
‡Including Australia, Canada, India, New Zealand, etc.

The numbers killed in World War II have been the subject of intense argument ever since. Most authorities now think that of the 30 million Soviets who bore arms, there were 13.6 million military deaths. This includes a battlefield deaths total of approximately 7.8 million, plus up to 2.5 million who died later of wounds received in battle and disease, and, of the 5.8 million who were taken prisoner, as many as 3.3 million who died in captivity. It should also be borne in mind that these were *military* losses. To these should be added many untold millions of civilian war deaths, while recent estimates have suggested an additional figure of up to 25 million civilian deaths as a result of Stalinist purges, which began just before the outbreak of war.

NAZI WAR CRIMINALS HANGED AT NUREMBERG

1   Joachim von Ribbentrop, 53, former Ambassador to Great Britain and Hitler's last Foreign Minister (the first to be hanged, at 1:02 a.m. on Oct 16, 1946)

2   Field Marshal Wilhelm von Keitel, 64, who had ordered the killing of 50 Allied air force officers after the Great Escape

3   General Ernst Kaltenbrunner, 44, SS and Gestapo leader

4   Reichminister Alfred Rosenberg, 53, ex-Minister for Occupied Eastern territories

5   Reichminister Hans Frank, 46, ex-Governor of Poland

6   Reichminister Wilhelm Frick, 69, former Minister of the Interior

7   Gauleiter Julius Streicher, 61, editor of anti-Semitic magazine *Die Stürmer*

8   Reichminister Fritz Sauckel, 52, ex-General Plenipotentiary for the Utilization of Labor (the slave-labor program)

9   Colonel General Alfred Jodl, 56, former Chief of the General Staff

10 Gauleiter Artur von Seyss-Inquart, 53, Governor of Austria and later Commissioner for Occupied Holland (the last to be hanged)

The International Military Tribunal trials (November 20, 1945, to August 31, 1946) sentenced 12 to death. Martin Bormann had escaped and Hermann Goering committed suicide, but the remaining 10 were hanged at Nuremberg Prison on October 16, 1946.

MOST POPULATED COUNTRIES

	Country	Percentage of world total	Population, estimated 2010
1	China	19.62	1,347,563,498
2	India	17.24	1,184,090,490
3	USA	4.50	309,162,581
4	Indonesia	3.54	242,968,342
5	Brazil	2.93	201,103,330
6	Pakistan	2.62	179,659,223
7	Bangladesh	2.33	159,765,367
8	Nigeria	2.22	152,217,341
9	Russia	2.03	139,390,205
10	Japan	1.85	126,804,433
	Top 10 total	*58.87*	*4,042,724,810*
	World total	*100*	*6,866,880,431*

Source: US Census Bureau, International Data Base

In 2009, the population of Nigeria overtook that of Russia, the only country in the Top 10 whose population is declining. Mexico, with a projected 2010 population of 112,468,855, is the only other country in the world with a population of more than 100 million.

TOP 10
LEAST POPULATED COUNTRIES

	Country	Population, estimated 2010
1	Vatican City	557
2	Tuvalu	12,576
3	Nauru	14,264
4	Palau	20,879
5	San Marino	30,235
6	Monaco	33,095
7	Liechtenstein	35,002
8	Saint Kitts and Nevis	40,498
9	Marshall Islands	65,859
10	Antigua and Barbuda	86,754

Source: US Census Bureau, International Data Base

The most recent and unusually precise official statistics published by Vatican City in 2007 revealed that the resident population comprised the Pope and 57 cardinals, 293 clergy members of pontifical representations, 62 other clergy, 101 members of the Swiss Guard, and 43 other lay persons. Only those employed by the Holy See can acquire citizenship, which is relinquished when their employment is terminated, but they may then be granted Italian citizenship.

US STATES WHERE MEN MOST OUTNUMBER WOMEN

	State	Men	Women	Ratio*
1	Alaska	357,607	328,686	**108.7**
2	Nevada	1,324,590	1,275,577	**103.8**
3	Wyoming	270,190	262,478	**102.9**
4	Utah	1,381,261	1,355,163	**101.9**
5=	Colorado	2,491,041	2,448,415	**101.7**
=	Hawaii	649,519	638,679	**101.7**
7	Idaho	766,580	757,236	**101.2**
8	North Dakota	321,933	319,548	**100.7**
9	Arizona	3,256,691	3,243,489	**100.4**
10	Montana	484,485	482,955	**100.3**

*Males per 100 females
Source: US Census Bureau

US STATES WHERE WOMEN MOST OUTNUMBER MEN

	State	Women	Men	Ratio*
1	Maryland	2,906,274	2,727,323	**106.7**
2=	Rhode Island	542,083	508,705	**106.5**
=	Alabama	2,403,813	2,258,087	**106.5**
4	Mississippi	1,514,777	1,423,841	**106.4**
5	Delaware	449,756	423,336	**106.2**
6	Massachusetts	3,344,791	3,153,176	**106.1**
7=	New York	10,028,234	9,462,063	**106.0**
=	Louisiana	2,269,998	2,140,798	**106.0**
9=	Pennsylvania	6,388,109	6,060,170	**105.4**
=	South Carolina	2,298,522	2,181,278	**105.4**

*Females per 100 males
Source: US Census Bureau

LARGEST COUNTRIES

	Country	Area	Percentage of world total
1	Russia	6,601,169 sq miles (17,098,242 sq km)	**11.5**
2	Canada	3,855,103 sq miles (9,984,670 sq km)	**6.7**
3	USA	3,794,101 sq miles (9,826,675 sq km)	**6.6**
4	China	3,705,408 sq miles (9,596,961 sq km)	**6.4**
5	Brazil	3,287,613 sq miles (8,514,877 sq km)	**5.7**
6	Australia	2,988,902 sq miles (7,741,220 sq km)	**5.2**
7	India	1,269,219 sq miles (3,287,263 sq km)	**2.2**
8	Argentina	1,073,519 sq miles (2,780,400 sq km)	**2.1**
9	Kazakhstan	1,052,090 sq miles (2,724,900 sq km)	**1.9**
10	Sudan	967,500 sq miles (2,505,813 sq km)	**1.7**
	World total	*57,506,062 sq miles (148,940,000 sq km)*	*100*

Source: CIA, *The World Factbook 2009*

This list is based on the total area of a country within its borders, including offshore islands and inland water such as lakes, rivers, and reservoirs. It may thus differ from versions in which these are excluded. Antarctica has an approximate area of 5,405,431 sq miles (14,000,000 sq km), but is discounted as it is not considered a country. The countries in the Top 10 collectively comprise 50 percent of the total Earth's surface.

SMALLEST COUNTRIES

	Country	Area
1	Vatican City	0.17 sq miles (0.44 sq km)
2	Monaco	0.75 sq miles (1.95 sq km)
3	Nauru	8.18 sq miles (21.20 sq km)
4	Tuvalu	9.89 sq miles (25.63 sq km)
5	San Marino	23.63 sq miles (61.20 sq km)
6	Liechtenstein	61.77 sq miles (160 sq km)
7	Marshall Islands	70.05 sq miles (181.43 sq km)
8	Saint Kitts and Nevis	104.01 sq miles (269.40 sq km)
9	Maldives	115.05 sq miles (298 sq km)
10	Malta	121.66 sq miles (315.10 sq km)

There are some 25 "microstates"—independent countries with an area of less than 386 sq miles (1,000 sq km). The "country" status of the Vatican is questionable, since its government and other features are intricately linked with those of Italy. The Vatican did become part of unified Italy in the 19th century, but its identity as an independent state was recognized by a treaty of February 11, 1929. If it is discounted, Grenada (132.81 sq miles/344 sq km) would join the list.

LONGEST PLACE NAMES*

Name	Letters

1 Krung Thep Mahanakhon Amon Rattanakosin **168**
Mahinthara Ayuthaya Mahadilok Phop Noppharat
Ratchathani Burirom Udomratchaniwet Mahasathan
Amon Piman Awatan Sathit Sakkathattiya Witsanukam
Prasit

It means "The city of angels, the great city, the eternal jewel city, the impregnable city of God Indra, the grand capital of the world endowed with nine precious gems, the happy city, abounding in an enormous royal palace that resembles the heavenly abode where reigns the reincarnated god, a city given by Indra and built by Vishnukarn." When the poetic name of Bangkok, capital of Thailand, is used, it is usually abbreviated to "Krung Thep" (city of angels).

2 Taumatawhakatangihangakoauauotamate- **85**
aturipukakapiki-maungahoronukupokaiwhen-
uakitanatahu

This is the longer version (the other has a mere 83 letters) of the Maori name of a hill in New Zealand. It translates as "The place where Tamatea, the man with the big knees, who slid, climbed, and swallowed mountains, known as land-eater, played on the flute to his loved one."

3 Gorsafawddachaidraigddanheddogle- **67**
ddollônpenrhyn-areurdraethceredigion

A name contrived by the Fairbourne Steam Railway, Gwynedd, North Wales, for publicity purposes and in order to outdo its rival, No. 4. It means "The Mawddach station and its dragon teeth at the Northern Penrhyn Road on the golden beach of Cardigan Bay."

4 Llanfairpwllgwyngyllgogerychwyrndrob- **58**
wllllantysilio-gogogoch

This is the place in Gwynedd famed especially for the length of its railroad tickets. It means "St. Mary's Church in the hollow of the white hazel near to the rapid whirlpool of the church of St. Tysilo near the Red Cave." Questions have been raised about its authenticity, since its official name comprises only the first 20 letters, and the full name appears to have been invented as a hoax in the 19th century by a local tailor.

5 El Pueblo de Nuestra Señora la Reina de los Ángeles **57**
   de la Porciúncula

The site of a Franciscan mission and the full Spanish name of Los Angeles, it means "The town of Our Lady the Queen of the Angels of the Little Portion." Nowadays it is customarily known by its initial letters, "LA," making it also one of the shortest-named cities in the world.

6 Chargoggagoggmanchauggagoggchaubunagungamaugg **45**

America's longest place name, a lake near Webster, Massachusetts. Its Indian name, loosely translated, is claimed to mean "You fish on your side, I'll fish on mine, and no one fishes in the middle." It is said to be pronounced "Char-gogg-a-gogg (pause) man-chaugg-a-gog (pause) chau-bun-a-gung-a-maug." It is, however, an invented extension of its real name (Chabunagungamaug, or "boundary fishing place"), devised in the 1920s by Larry Daly, the editor of the *Webster Times*.

7= Lower North Branch Little Southwest Miramichi **40**

Canada's longest place name—a short river in New Brunswick.

= Villa Real de la Santa Fé de San Francisco de Asis **40**

The full Spanish name of Santa Fe, New Mexico, translates as "Royal city of the holy faith of St. Francis of Assisi."

9 Te Whakatakanga-o-te-ngarehu-o-te-ahi-a-Tamatea **38**

The Maori name of Hammer Springs, New Zealand. Like No. 2 on this list, it refers to a legend of Tamatea, explaining how the springs were warmed by "the falling of the cinders of the fire of Tamatea." Its name is variously written either hyphenated or as a single word.

10 Meallan Liath Coire Mhic Dhubhghaill **32**

The longest multiple name in Scotland, a place near Aultanrynie, Highland, alternatively spelled Meallan Liath Coire Mhic Dhughaill (30 letters).

*Including single-word, hyphenated, and multiple names

LONGEST PLACE NAMES IN THE USA*

	Name/location	Letters
1	Chargoggagoggmanchauggagogg-chaubunagungamaugg, Massachusetts[†]	45
2	Nunathloogagamiutbingoi Dunes, Alaska	23
3=	Kleinfeltersville, Pennsylvania	17
=	Mooselookmeguntic, Maine	17
5=	Chancellorsville, Virginia	16
=	Chickasawhatchee, Georgia	16
=	Eichelbergertown, Pennsylvania	16
=	Nollidewabticook, Maine	16
9	Pongowayhaymock, Maine	15
10	Anasagunticook, Maine	14

*Single only, excluding hyphenated names
†See Top 10 Longest Place Names, No. 6
Source: US Geological Survey Geographical Names Information System (GNIS)

The longest hyphenated names in the US are Winchester-on-the-Severn, Maryland, and Washington-on-the-Brazos, Texas, both of which contain 21 letters. A number of long American place names are of Native American origin, but some are not as long as they once were: in 1916 the US Board on Geographic Names saw fit to reduce the 26-letter New Hampshire stream known as Quohquinapassakessamanagno to "Beaver Creek," while the Conamabsqunooncant River became "Duck." Among the shortest US place names are several with just two letters. These are especially prevalent in Kentucky, which boasts an Ed, Ep, Or, Oz, and Uz.

MOST COMMON PLACE NAMES IN THE USA

	Name*	Populated places
1	Midway	218
2	Fairview	213
3	Oak Grove	169
4	Five Points	150
5	Riverside	129
6	Pleasant Hill	124
7	Mount Pleasant	119
8	Bethel	111
9	Centerville	109
10	New Hope	108

*Exact names only, excluding variants
Source: US Geological Survey Geographic Names Information System (GNIS)

Fairview figures prominently in certain states—there are 27 in Tennessee alone. It is also one of the most common cemetery names in the US, with no fewer than 60 examples; there are also 88 cemeteries called Riverside and 43 called Oak Grove. Springfield, the home of *The Simpsons*, is sometimes claimed as America's most common name, but the USGS records just 67 examples in 33 states.

MOST COMMON STREET NAMES IN THE USA

	Street	Total
1	Second Street	10,866
2	Third Street	10,131
3	First Street	9,898
4	Fourth Street	9,190
5	Park Street	8,926
6	Fifth Street	8,186
7	Main Street	7,664
8	Sixth Street	7,283
9	Oak Street	6,946
10	Seventh Street	6,377

Source: US Census Bureau

First is not first, because many streets that would be so designated are instead called Main. Washington is the highest-ranked street name derived from a personal name, with 4,974 examples.

TOP 10

TALLEST HABITABLE BUILDINGS

	Building/location	Year completed	Stories	Height
1	Burj Dubai, Dubai, UAE	2009	162	2,684 ft (818 m)
2	Taipei 101, Taipei, Taiwan	2004	101	1,470 ft (448 m)
3	Shanghai World Financial Center Shanghai, China	2008	101	1,614 ft (492 m)
4	International Commerce Centre, Hong Kong, China	2010*	118	1,588 ft (484 m)
5	Abraj Al Bait Towers, Mecca, Saudi Arabia	2010*	76	1,509 ft (460 m)
6	Petronas Towers, Kuala Lumpur, Malaysia	1998	88	1,483 ft (452 m)
7	Willis Tower[†], Chicago, USA	1973	110	1,451 ft (442 m)
8	West Tower, Guangzhou, China	2009	110	1,417 ft (432 m)[‡]
9	Jin Mao Building, Shanghai, China	1998	88	1,255 ft (383 m)
10	Trump International Hotel and Tower, Chicago, USA	2009	96	1,362 ft (415 m)

*Under construction, scheduled completion date
†Formerly Sears Tower
‡Helipad takes height to 1,435 ft (437.5 m)

TALLEST HABITABLE BUILDINGS IN THE USA*

	Building/location	Year completed	Stories	Roof height
1	Willis Tower†, Chicago, Illinois	1973	110	1,451 ft (442 m)
2	Trump International Hotel and Tower, Chicago, Illinois	2009	92	1,362 ft (415 m)
3	Empire State Building, New York, New York	1931	102	1,250 ft (381 m)
4	Bank of America Tower New York, New York	2009	54	1,198 ft (365 m)
5	Aon Center, Chicago, Illinois	1973	83	1,136 ft (346 m)
6	John Hancock Center, Chicago, Illinois	1969	100	1,127 ft (344 m)
7	Chrysler Building New York, New York	1930	77	1,046 ft (319 m)
8	US Bank Tower, Los Angeles, California	1990	73	1,018 ft (310 m)
9	AT&T Corporate Center, Chicago, Illinois	1989	60	1,007 ft (307 m)
10	JP Morgan Chase Tower, Houston, Texas	1982	75	1,002 ft (305 m)

*Buildings completed or topped out, excluding communications masts, towers, chimneys, and church spires
†Formerly Sears Tower
Source: Council on Tall Buildings and Urban Habitat

LONGEST SUSPENSION BRIDGES

	Bridge/location	Year completed	Length of main span
1	Akashi-Kaikyo, Kobe-Naruto, Japan	1998	6,532 ft (1,991 m)
2	Xihoumen, China	2007	5,413 ft (1,650 m)
3	Great Belt, Denmark	1997	5,328 ft (1,624 m)
4	Ryungyang, China	2005	4,888 ft (1,490 m)
5	Humber Estuary, UK	1980	4,625 ft (1,410 m)
6	Jiangyin, China	1998	4,543 ft (1,385 m)
7	Tsing Ma, Hong Kong, China	1997	4,518 ft (1,377 m)
8	Verrazano-Narrows, New York, USA	1964	4,260 ft (1,298 m)
9=	Golden Gate, San Francisco, USA	1937	4,200 ft (1,280 m)
=	Yangluo, China	2007	4,200 ft (1,280 m)

The planned Messina Strait Bridge between Sicily and Calabria, Italy, would have had the longest center span of any bridge at 10,827 ft (3,300 m), but the project was canceled on October 11, 2006.

TOP 10
LONGEST RAIL TUNNELS

	Tunnel/location	Year completed	Length
1	AlpTransit Gotthard, Switzerland	2018*	35.6 miles (57.1 km)
2	Seikan, Japan	1988	33.6 miles (53.9 km)
3	Channel Tunnel, France/England	1994	31.5 miles (50.5 km)
4	Moscow Metro (Serpukhovsko-Timiryazevskaya line), Russia	2002	25.9 miles (41.5 km)
5	Moscow Metro (Kaluzhsko--Rizhskaya line), Russia	1990	23.4 miles (37.6 km)
6	Lötschberg Base, Switzerland	2007	21.6 miles (34.6 km)
7	Berlin U-Bahn (U7 line)	1984	19.8 miles (31.8 km)
8	Guadarrama, Spain	2007	17.7 miles (28.4 km)
9	Taihang, China	2008	17.4 miles (27.9 km)
10	London Underground (East Finchley-Morden, Northern Line), UK	1939	17.3 miles (27.8 km)

*Under construction, scheduled completion date

LONGEST ROAD TUNNELS

	Tunnel/location	Year completed	Length
1	Lærdal, Norway	2000	80,413 ft (24,510 m)
2	Zhongnanshan, China	2007	59,186 ft (18,040 m)
3	St. Gotthard, Switzerland	1980	55,505 ft (16,918 m)
4	Arlberg, Austria	1978	45,850 ft (13,972 m)
5	Hsuehshan, Taiwan	2006	42,323 ft (12,900 m)
6	Fréjus, France/Italy	1980	42,306 ft (12,895 m)
7	Mont-Blanc, France/Italy	1965	38,094 ft (11,611 m)
8	Gudvangen, Norway	1991	37,493 ft (11,428 m)
9	Folgefonn, Norway	2001	36,417 ft (11,100 m)
10	Kan-Etsu II (southbound), Japan	1991	36,122 ft (11,010 m)

The 13,780-ft (4,200-m) Ted Williams/Interstate 190 Extension Tunnel, Boston, Massachusetts (1995–2003), is the USA's longest road tunnel, while the 13,727-ft (4,184 m) Anton Anderson, Memorial Tunnel, Alaska, is America's longest combined rail and road tunnel. The Eisenhower-Johnson Memorial Tunnel, Colorado, is at 11,158 ft (3,401 m) the highest road tunnel in the world.

ONLINE LANGUAGES

	Language	Percentage of all Internet users	Internet users*
1	English	28.7	478,717,443
2	Chinese (Mandarin)	21.7	361,364,613
3	Spanish	8.0	132,963,898
4	Japanese	5.6	94,000,000
5	French	4.6	76,915,917
6	Portuguese	4.4	73,027,400
7	German	3.9	65,243,673
8	Arabic	3.0	49,372,400
9	Russian	2.3	38,000,000
10	Korean	2.2	37,475,800
	Top 10 languages	*84.3*	*1,407,081,144*
	Rest of world languages	*15.7*	*261,789,264*
	World total	*100*	*1,668,870,408*

*As of June 30, 2009
Source: www.internetworldstats.com

MOST-SPOKEN LANGUAGES*

	Language	Speakers
1	Chinese (Mandarin)	845,456,760
2	Spanish	328,518,810
3	English	328,008,138
4	Arabic	221,002,544
5	Hindi	181,676,620
6	Bengali	181,272,900
7	Portuguese	177,981,570
8	Russian	143,553,950
9	Japanese	122,080,100
10	German	90,294,110

*Primary speakers only
Source: M. Paul Lewis (ed.), *Ethnologue: Languages of the World*, sixteenth edition (Dallas, Texas: SIL International, 2009). Online version: http://www.ethnologue.com

LONGEST WORDS IN AMERICAN DICTIONARIES*

Word	Letters
1 Pneumonoultramicroscopicsilicovolcanoconiosis A lung disease caused by breathing in volcanic dust.	45
2 Supercalifragilisticexpialidocious Meaning "wonderful," from song of this title in the movie *Mary Poppins*.	34
3= Floccinaucinihilipilification Meaning "the action or habit of estimating as worthless."	29
= Trinitrophenylmethylnitramine[†] A chemical compound used as a detonator in shells.	29
5 Antidisestablishmentarianism Meaning "opposition to the disestablishment of the Church of England."	28
6= Electroencephalographically Relating to brain waves.	27
= Microspectrophotometrically Relating to the measurement of light waves.	27
8= Immunoelectrophoretically Relating to measurement of immunoglobulin.	25
= Spectroheliokinematograph A 1930s device for monitoring and filming solar activity.	25
= Syngenesiotransplantation Tissue graft.	25

*Excluding plurals and hyphenated forms
†Several other chemical compound names are of similar length
Source: Chris Cole, editor of rec.puzzles archive

TOP 10

OLDEST UNIVERSITIES AND COLLEGES IN THE USA

	University/location	Year chartered
1	Harvard University, Massachusetts	1636
2	College of William and Mary, Virginia	1692
3	Yale University, Connecticut	1701
4	University of Pennsylvania, Pennsylvania	1740
5	Moravian College, Pennsylvania	1742
6	Princeton University, New Jersey	1746
7	Washington and Lee University, Virginia	1749
8	Columbia University, New York	1754
9	Brown University, Rhode Island	1764
10	Rutgers, the State University of New Jersey	1766

Source: National Center for Education Statistics

BEST-SELLING ENGLISH-LANGUAGE NOVELS

Book/first published	Minimum estimated sales*
1 J. R. R. Tolkien, *The Lord of the Rings*, 1954–55	150,000,000
2 J. K. Rowling, *Harry Potter and the Philosopher's Stone*, 1997	120,000,000
3= J. R. R. Tolkien, *The Hobbit*, 1937	100,000,000
= Agatha Christie, *And Then There Were None*, 1939	100,000,000
5 Dan Brown, *The Da Vinci Code*, 2003	80,000,000
6 J. K. Rowling, *Harry Potter and the Chamber of Secrets*, 1998	77,000,000
7 J. K. Rowling, *Harry Potter and the Goblet of Fire*, 2000	66,000,000
8= J. D. Salinger, *The Catcher in the Rye*, 1951	65,000,000
= J. K. Rowling, *Harry Potter and the Half-Blood Prince*, 2005	65,000,000
10 J. K. Rowling, *Harry Potter and the Prisoner of Azkaban*, 1999	60,000,000

*Including translations

BOOKS FOUND IN MOST US LIBRARIES

	Book	Total library holdings*
1	The Bible	796,882
2	*US Census*	460,628
3	*Mother Goose*	67,663
4	Dante Alighieri, *Divine Comedy*	62,414
5	Homer, *The Odyssey*	45,551
6	Homer, *The Iliad*	44,093
7	Mark Twain, *Huckleberry Finn*	42,724
8	J. R. R. Tolkien, *Lord of the Rings* (trilogy)	40,907
9	William Shakespeare, *Hamlet*	39,521
10	Lewis Carroll, *Alice's Adventures in Wonderland*	39,277

*Based on WorldCat listings of all editions of books held in 53,000 libraries in the USA and other countries
Source: OCLC (Online Computer Library Center)

TOP 10
INTERNET SEARCH SUBJECTS*

1 Britney Spears
2 WWE (World Wrestling Entertainment)
3 Barack Obama
4 Miley Cyrus
5 RuneScape
6 Jessica Alba
7 Naruto
8 Lindsay Lohan
9 Angelina Jolie
10 American Idol

*For 2008
Source: Yahoo!

MOST VISITED
WEBSITES IN THE USA*

1   Google: google.com

2   Yahoo!: yahoo.com

3   Facebook: facebook.com

4   YouTube: youtube.com

5   Myspace: myspace.com

6   Windows Live: live.com

7   Wikipedia: wikipedia.org

8   Craigslist: craigslist.org

9   eBay: ebay.com

10   Microsoft Network (MSN): msn.com

*Based on Alexa traffic rankings

Founded in 1996, California-based Internet information company Alexa was acquired by Amazon.com in 1999. Its traffic rankings are widely regarded as providing the most accurate snapshot of the world's most visited websites and indicate the variations from country to country.

TOP 10
OLDEST NEWSPAPERS IN THE USA

	Newspaper/city	Founded
1	*The Hartford Courant*, Hartford, Connecticut	**1764**
2=	*Poughkeepsie Journal*, Poughkeepsie, New York	**1785**
=	*The Augusta Chronicle*, Augusta, Georgia	**1785**
=	*The Register Star*, Hudson, New York	**1785**
5=	*Pittsburgh Post-Gazette*, Pittsburgh, Pennsylvania	**1786**
=	*Daily Hampshire Gazette*, Northampton, Massachusetts	**1786**
7	*The Berkshire Eagle*, Pittsfield, Massachusetts	**1789**
8	*Norwich Bulletin*, Norwich, Connecticut	**1791**
9	*The Recorder*, Greenfield, Massachusetts	**1792**
10	*Intelligencer Journal*, Lancaster, Pennsylvania	**1794**

Source: *Editor and Publisher Year Book*

Among even older newspapers that are no longer extant is the *Boston News-Letter*, first published in 1704 by New England postmaster John Campbell. It measured just 7.5 x 12 in (19 x 30.5 cm) and had a circulation of 300 copies.

PRINT MEDIA

DAILY NEWSPAPERS IN THE USA

	Newspaper	Average daily circulation*
1	*USA Today*	2,113,725
2	*The Wall Street Journal*	2,082,189
3	*The New York Times*	1,039,031
4	*Los Angeles Times*	723,181
5	*Washington Post*	665,383
6	*New York Daily News*	602,857
7	*Houston Chronicle*	558,140
8	*Chicago Tribune*	501,202
9	*New York Post*	425,138
10	*Arizona Republic*	389,701

*Daily average for six months to March 31, 2009
Source: Audit Bureau of Circulations

SUNDAY NEWSPAPERS IN THE USA

	Newspaper	Average Sunday circulation*
1	The New York Times	1,451,233
2	Los Angeles Times	1,019,388
3	Washington Post	868,965
4	Chicago Tribune	858,256
5	New York News	644,766
6	Detroit News & Free Press	585,022
7	Houston Chronicle	583,364
8	Philadelphia Inquirer	550,400
9	The Denver Post/Rocky Mountain News	540,147
10	The Boston Globe	466,665

*Sunday average for six months to March 31, 2009
Source: Audit Bureau of Circulations

SUBJECTS IN US MAGAZINES*

	Subject	Percentage of pages	Number of pages
1	Entertainment/celebrity	15.8	28,496.0
2	Wearing apparel/accessories	12.1	21,835.6
3	Travel/transportation	8.4	15,178.4
4	Home furnishings/management	8.3	14,998.0
5	Food/nutrition	7.2	12,943.4
6	Culture	6.3	11,279.1
7	Business/industry	5.7	10,281.1
8	Sports/recreation/hobby	4.6	8,367.6
9	Health/medical science	4.4	7,934.3
10	Beauty and grooming	4.1	7,350.3
	Top 10 total	*76.9*	*138,663.8*
	Total (including categories outside Top 10)	*100*	*180,066.8*

*Based on a survey of 160 US magazines during 2007
Source: Hall's Magazine Reports/Magazine Publishers of America, *The Magazine Handbook 2009–2010*

MAGAZINES IN THE USA

	Magazine	Average circulation*
1	*Reader's Digest*	8,158,652
2	*Better Homes and Gardens*	7,634,197
3	*National Geographic*	4,708,307
4	*Family Circle*	3,932,510
5	*Good Housekeeping*	4,630,397
6	*Woman's Day*	3,933,990
7	*Ladies' Home Journal*	3,842,791
8	*People*	3,615,858
9	*Game Informer*	3,601,201
10	*Prevention*	3,312,624

*Paid circulation only (excluding free magazines, circulation to membership organizations, etc.), 2009
Source: Audit Bureau of Circulations

MEN'S MAGAZINES IN THE USA

	Magazine	Average circulation*
1	*Sports Illustrated*	3,239,968
2	*Playboy*	2,658,885
3	*Maxim*	2,528,797
4	*American Legion Magazine*	2,472,955
5	*ESPN The Magazine*	2,053,770
6	*Men's Health*	1,864,101
7	*Golf Digest*	1,652,435
8	*Field & Stream*	1,530,037
9	*Golf Magazine*	1,412,994
10	*American Rifleman*	1,394,357

*2008
Source: Audit Bureau of Circulations

MOST VALUABLE AMERICAN COMIC BOOKS

	Comic/publisher	Value*
1	*Action Comics*, No. 1 (DC)	**$2,100,000**

Published in June 1938, the first issue of *Action Comics* marked the original appearance of Superman.

| 2 | *Detective Comics*, No. 27 (DC) | **$1,500,000** |

Issued in May 1939, it is prized as the first comic book to feature Batman.

| 3 | *Superman*, No. 1 (DC) | **$1,200,000** |

The first comic book devoted to Superman, published in Summer 1939.

| 4 | *All-American Comics*, No. 16 (All-American) | **$600,000** |

The Green Lantern made his debut in the issue dated July 1940

| 5 | *Marvel Comics*, No. 1 (Marvel) | **$540,000** |

The Human Torch was first introduced in the October 1939 issue.

| 6 | *Batman*, No. 1 (DC) | **$480,000** |

Published in Spring 1940, this was the first comic book devoted to Batman.

| 7 | *Captain America Comics*, No. 1 (Timely) | **$384,000** |

Captain America first appeared in the March 1941 issue.

| 8 | *Detective Comics*, No. 1 (DC) | **$312,000** |

Issued in March 1937, this was an anthology that featured detective Slam Bradley.

| 9 | *Flash Comics*, No. 1 (All-American) | **$276,000** |

Dated January 1940, and featuring The Flash, it is rare because it was produced in small numbers for promotional purposes.

| 10 | *Amazing Fantasy*, No. 15 (Marvel) | **$252,000** |

Spider-Man made his debut in the August 1962 issue.

*For example in "mint" or "near-mint" condition

LONGEST-RUNNING COMIC STRIPS IN THE USA

	Comic strip	First published
1	*Katzenjammer Kids*	Aug 12, 1897
2	*Gasoline Alley*	Nov 24, 1918
3	*Barney Google**	Jun 17, 1919
4	*Tarzan*	Jan 7, 1929
5	*Blondie*	Sep 8, 1930
6	*Dick Tracy*	Oct 4, 1931
7	*Alley Oop*	Aug 7, 1933
8	*The Phantom*	Feb 17, 1936
9	*Prince Valiant*	Feb 13, 1937
10	*Nancy*†	[1938‡]

Barney Google and Snuffy Smith from Oct 24, 1934
†Introduced in 1933 as a character in *Fritzi Ritz* (launched Oct 9, 1922); strip renamed *Nancy* in 1938
‡Precise date unknown

TOP 10

MOST EXPENSIVE ITEMS OF ROCK MEMORABILIA SOLD AT AUCTION

	Item/auction	Price*
1	John Lennon's 1965 Rolls-Royce Phantom V touring limousine, Sotheby's, New York, Jun 29, 1985	$2,299,000
2	John Lennon's Steinway Model Z upright piano, Fleetwood-Owen online auction, Hard Rock Café, London and New York, Oct 17, 2000	$2,100,000 (£1,450,000)
3	Beatles' 1967 *Sgt. Pepper's Lonely Hearts Club Band* painted drum skin, Christie's, London, Jul 10, 2008	$1,071,133 (£541,250)
4	Eric Clapton's 1956–57 "Blackie" Fender Stratocaster, Christie's, New York, Jun 24, 2004	$959,500
5	Jerry Garcia's "Tiger" guitar, Guernsey's at Studio 54, New York, May 8, 2002	$957,500
6	Eric Clapton's 1964 Gibson acoustic ES-335, Christie's, New York, Jun 24, 2004	$847,500
7	John Lennon's handwritten lyrics for "Give Peace a Chance," 1969, Christie's, London, Jul 10, 2008	$833,653 (£421,250)

8	Eric Clapton's 1939 Martin acoustic, Christie's, New York, Jun 24, 2004	**$791,500**
9	Jerry Garcia's "Wolf" guitar, Guernsey's at Studio 54, New York, May 8, 2002	**$789,500**
10	Stevie Ray Vaughan's/Eric Clapton's "Lenny" Fender Stratocaster, Christie's, New York, Jun 24, 2004	**$623,500**

*Including buyer's premium, where appropriate

One of the first auctions of rock memorabilia was held at the Fillmore East, New York on October 12, 1970, as a fundraiser for anti-war politicians. Sotheby's, the old-established London auction house, held the first major auction of rock memorabilia in December 1981. It has since become big business—especially if it involves personal association with mega-stars such as the Beatles. Although sold in 1985, John Lennon's psychedelically-painted Rolls-Royce (now in the Royal British Columbia Museum, Victoria, Canada) still heads the list, closely followed by the piano played by Lennon at Woodstock and on which he composed "Imagine," which was purchased by George Michael. Even such items as the Liverpool birthplace of Ringo Starr, the barber's shop mentioned in the Beatles song "Penny Lane," and a door from John Lennon's home have been offered for sale as artefacts from the archeology of the Beatles. Guitars owned by the world's great rock guitarists also figure prominently, in some instances changing hands several times as they have been re auctioned by a sequence of celebrity owners to raise money for charities. Close runners-up include handwritten lyrics, such as Bernie Taupin's for the rewritten "Candle in the Wind," sung by Elton John at the funeral of Princess Diana, and sold at Christie's, Los Angeles on February 11, 1998 for $400,000).

MOST EXPENSIVE ITEMS OF MOVIE MEMORABILIA SOLD AT AUCTION

	Item/auction	Price
1	Marilyn Monroe's beaded dress, worn May 19, 1962, when she sang "Happy Birthday, Mr. President" to John F. Kennedy, Christie's, New York, Oct 27, 1999	$1,267,500
2	Audrey Hepburn's black dress from *Breakfast at Tiffany's* (1961), Christie's, London, Dec 5, 2006	$923,187 (£467,000)
3	Judy Garland's ruby slippers from *The Wizard of Oz* (1939), Christie's, New York, May 26, 2000	$666,000
4	Marilyn Monroe's piano, Christie's, New York, Oct 27, 1999	$662,500
5	Clark Gable's Oscar for *It Happened One Night* (1934), Christie's, Los Angeles, Dec 15, 1996	$607,500
6	Vivien Leigh's Oscar for *Gone with the Wind* (1939), Sotheby's, New York, Dec 15, 1993	$562,500
7	Poster for *The Mummy* (1932), Sotheby's, New York, Mar 1, 1997	$453,500

8	Statue of the Maltese Falcon from *The Maltese Falcon* (1941), Christie's Rockefeller Center, New York, Dec 5, 1994	**$398,500**
9	Poster for *Metropolis* (1927), Sotheby's, New York, Oct 28, 2000	**$357,750**
10	James Bond's Aston Martin DB5 from *Goldfinger* (1964), Sotheby's, New York, Jun 28, 1986	**$275,000**

This list encompasses memorabilia related to movies and movie stars, but excludes animated movie celluloids or "cels"—the individually painted scenes that are shot in sequence to make up cartoon films. Among near-misses in the £100,000-plus league are Marlon Brando's script for *The Godfather* (1972), which made £173,373 in 2005; James Bond's Aston Martin DB5 from *GoldenEye* (1995), sold for £157,750 in 2001; Clark Gable's script for *Gone with the Wind*, which achieved £146,700 in 1996, the "Rosebud" sled from *Citizen Kane* (1941), £140,000 in 1996, and Herman J. Mankiewicz's scripts for this movie and an earlier draft (originally called "American"), £139,157 in 1989. Oscar statuettes are occasionally auctioned, but, since 1950, winners have signed agreements not to sell them, except back to the Academy of Motion Picture Arts and Sciences, for one dollar, in an attempt to prevent them from becoming collectables. The Oscar awarded to Clark Gable at No. 5 in the Top 10 was acquired by Steven Spielberg and returned to the Academy, as he did in 2001 with Bette Davis's Oscar for *Jezebel* (1938). In 2007, Orson Welles's Oscar for *Citizen Kane*, with a presale estimate of $1.2 million, failed to find a buyer at auction.

MOST EXPENSIVE PAINTINGS BY AMERICAN ARTISTS SOLD AT AUCTION

	Painting/artist/auction	Price
1	*White Center*, Mark Rothko, Sotheby's, New York, May 15, 2007	**$72,840,000**
2	*Green car crash–Green burning car I*, Andy Warhol, Christie's, New York, May 16, 2007	**$71,720,000**
3	*No. 15*, Mark Rothko, Christie's, New York, May 13, 2008	**$50,441,000**
4	*200 One Dollar Bills*, Andy Warhol, Sotheby's, New York, Nov 11, 2009	**$43,762,500**
5	*Untitled–Red, Blue, Orange*, Mark Rothko, Christie's, New York, Nov 13, 2007	**$34,201,000**
6	*Double Marlon*, Andy Warhol, Christie's, New York, May 13, 2008	**$32,521,000**
7	*Lemon Marilyn*, Andy Warhol, Christie's, New York, May 16, 2007	**$28,040,000**
8	*Polo Crowd*, George Wesley Bellows, Sotheby's, New York, Dec 1, 1999	**$27,702,500**
9	*Untitled XXV*, Willem de Kooning*, Christie's, New York, Nov 15, 2006	**$27,120,000**
10	*Untitled*, Mark Rothko, Christie's, New York, May 16, 2007	**$26,920,000**

*Dutch-born, naturalized US citizen

MOST EXPENSIVE PAINTINGS SOLD AT AUCTION

Painting/artist/auction	Price
1 *Garçon à la pipe*, Pablo Picasso, Sotheby's, New York, May 5, 2004	$104,168,000
2 *Dora Maar au chat*, Pablo Picasso, Sotheby's, New York, May 3, 2006	$95,216,000
3 *Portrait of Adele Bloch-Bauer II*, Gustav Klimt, Christie's, New York, Nov 8, 2006	$87,936,000
4 *Triptych*, Francis Bacon, Sotheby's, New York, May 14, 2008	$86,281,000
5 *Portrait du Docteur Gachet*, Vincent van Gogh, Christie's, New York, May 15, 1990	$82,500,000
6 *Le Bassin aux Nymphéas*, Claude Monet, Christie's, London, Jun 24, 2008	$80,379,591 (£40,921,250)
7 *Bal au Moulin de la Galette, Montmartre*, Pierre-Auguste Renoir, Sotheby's, New York, May 17, 1990	$78,100,000
8 *The Massacre of the Innocents*, Sir Peter Paul Rubens, Sotheby's, London, Jul 10, 2002	$75,930,440 (£49,506,648)
9 *White Center*, Mark Rothko, Sotheby's, New York, May 15, 2007	$72,840,000
10 *Green car crash–Green burning car I*, Andy Warhol, Christie's, New York, May 16, 2007	$71,720,000

*Including buyer's premium

MOST EXPENSIVE CARS SOLD AT AUCTION

	Car/auction	Price
1	1957 Ferrari 250 TR, RM Auctions, Maranello, Italy, May 17, 2009	$12,402,500
2	1961 Ferrari 250 GT, RM Auctions, Maranello, Italy, May 18, 2008	$10,894,400
3	1962 Ferrari GTO, Sotheby's, Monte Carlo, Monaco, May 21, 1990	$10,800,000
4	1931 Bugatti Royale Type 41 Chassis "41.141," Christie's, London (at the Royal Albert Hall), England, Nov 19, 1987	$9,800,000
5	1962 Ferrari 330 TRI/LM Testa Rossa, RM Auctions, Maranello, Italy, May 20, 2007	$9,281,250
6	1937 Mercedes-Benz 540K, RM Auctions, London, England, Oct 31, 2007	$8,235,112
7	1937 Bugatti Type 57SC, Gooding & Co, Pebble Beach, California, Aug 13, 2008	$7,920,000
8	1965 Shelby Daytona Cobra, Mecum Auctions, Monterey, California, Aug 15, 2009	$7,685,000
9	1929 Mercedes-Benz 38/250 SSK, Bonhams, Chichester, England, Sep 3, 2004	$7,443,070
10	1904 Rolls-Royce 10hp two-seater, Bonhams, Olympia, London, England, Dec 3, 2007	$7,254,290

TOP 10
SINGLES OF ALL TIME

	Title/artist or group	Year	Sales exceed
1	"Candle in the Wind (1997)/ Something About the Way You Look Tonight," Elton John	1997	**37,000,000**
2	"White Christmas," Bing Crosby	1942	**30,000,000**
3	"Rock Around the Clock," Bill Haley and His Comets	1954	**17,000,000**
4	"I Want to Hold Your Hand," The Beatles	1963	**12,000,000**
5=	"It's Now or Never," Elvis Presley	1960	**10,000,000**
=	"Hey Jude," The Beatles	1968	**10,000,000**
=	"I Will Always Love You," Whitney Houston	1992	**10,000,000**
8=	"Diana," Paul Anka	1957	**9,000,000**
=	"Hound Dog/Don't Be Cruel," Elvis Presley	1956	**9,000,000**
10=	"(Everything I Do) I Do It for You," Bryan Adams	1991	**8,000,000**
=	"I'm a Believer," The Monkees	1966	**8,000,000**

Source: Music Information Database

SINGLES OF ALL TIME IN THE USA

	Title/artist or group/release	Estimated US sales*
1	"Candle in the Wind (1997)/Something About the Way You Look Tonight," Elton John (1997)	11,000,000
2	"White Christmas," Bing Crosby (1942)	8,000,000
3	"Low," Flo Rida (2007)	5,000,000
4=	"Hound Dog/Don't Be Cruel," Elvis Presley (1953)	4,000,000
=	"Hey Jude," The Beatles (1968)	4,000,000
=	"We Are the World," USA for Africa (1985)	4,000,000
=	"I Will Always Love You," Whitney Houston (1992)	4,000,000
=	"Whoomp! (There it Is)," Tag Team (1993)	4,000,000
=	"I'm Yours," Jason Mraz (2008)	4,000,000
=	"Love Story," Taylor Swift (2008)	4,000,000

*Includes digital downloads
Source: RIAA

The USA for Africa's 1985 charity single "We Are the World" had a host of special circumstances surrounding it, which launched it into the elite 4-million mega-seller league. It took the remarkable global response to the death of Diana, Princess of Wales, to generate sales capable of overtaking it, which Elton John's specially penned tribute did—and by a considerable margin.

ALBUMS OF ALL TIME

Album/artist or group/year	Sales (millions) USA	World total
1 *Thriller*, Michael Jackson (1982)	29	110
2 *Back in Black*, AC/DC (1980)	22	49
3= *The Dark Side of The Moon*, Pink Floyd (1973)	15	43
= *Bat Out of Hell*, Meat Loaf (1978)	14	43
5= *Their Greatest Hits 1971–1975* Eagles (1976)	29	42
= *The Bodyguard* (soundtrack) (1992)	17	42
= *Dirty Dancing*, various artists (1987)	11	42
8= *Rumours*, Fleetwood Mac (1977)	19	40
= *Phantom of the Opera*, cast recording (1986)	4	40
= *Millennium*, Backstreet Boys (1999)	13	40

ALBUMS IN THE USA

	Album/artist or group/year	Estimated sales
1=	*Their Greatest Hits, 1971–1975*, Eagles (1976)	**29,000,000**
=	*Thriller*, Michael Jackson (1982)	**29,000,000**
3	*Led Zeppelin IV*, Led Zeppelin (1971)	**23,000,000**
4	*Back in Black*, AC/DC (1980)	**22,000,000**
5	*Come on Over*, Shania Twain (1997)	**20,000,000**
6	*Rumours*, Fleetwood Mac (1977)	**19,000,000**
7	*Appetite for Destruction*, Guns N' Roses (1987)	**18,000,000**
8=	*Boston*, Boston (1976)	**17,000,000**
=	*No Fences*, Garth Brooks (1990)	**17,000,000**
=	*The Bodyguard*, Soundtrack (1992)	**17,000,000**

Source: RIAA

The Eagles' *Their Greatest Hits, 1971–1975* was the first album ever to be certified platinum, (for sales of over one million copies) and long vied with Jackson's *Thriller* as the US's all-time No. 1. The list excludes double albums, such as Pink Floyd's *The Wall* (1979): RIAA certification counts each album separately, so although it has been certified 23 times platinum, its total US sales are 11.5 million.

MALE ARTISTS WITH MOST PLATINUM AND MULTI-PLATINUM ALBUMS (US)

	Artist	Platinum albums*
1	Garth Brooks (16)	106
2	Elvis Presley (82)	90
3=	Billy Joel (18)	68
=	Michael Jackson (10)	68
5	Elton John (38)	63
6	Bruce Springsteen (21)	54
7	George Strait (39)	53
8	Kenny G (15)	46
9	Kenny Rogers (31)	41
10	Neil Diamond (40)	39

*By number of album awards, rather than number of albums qualifying for awards; gold totals in brackets
Source: RIAA

Platinum singles and albums in the USA are those that have achieved sales of one million units. The award has been made by the Recording Industry Association of America (RIAA) since 1976, when it was introduced in response to escalating music sales, as a result of which many disks were outselling the 500,000 required to achieve a Gold Award. In 1984, the RIAA introduced Multi-Platinum Awards for certified sales of two million or more units.

MALE GUITARISTS*

1   Jimi Hendrix (1942–70)

2   Duane Allman (1946–71)

3   B.B. King (b.1925)

4   Eric Clapton (UK, b.1945)

5   Robert Johnson (1911–38)

6   Chuck Berry (b.1926)

7   Stevie Ray Vaughan (1954–90)

8   Ry Cooder (b.1947)

9   Jimmy Page (UK, b.1944)

10   Keith Richards (UK, b.1943)

*All from the USA, except where otherwise indicated
Source: *Rolling Stone*

This is the Top 10 of the list of "100 Greatest Guitarists of All Time" as published by *Rolling Stone* magazine. Between 2003 and 2008, *Rolling Stone* listed artists, songs, albums, and performances in a variety of categories, ranked according to votes cast by their peers—fellow musicians, critics, and prominent music industry figures.

HIGHEST-EARNING MOVIES IN THE WORLD

	Movie/year	Gross income	
		US	Total world
1	*Titanic*, 1997*	$600,788,188	**$1,848,813,795**
2	*The Lord of the Rings: The Return of the King*, 2003*	$377,027,325	**$1,129,219,252**
3	*Pirates of the Caribbean: Dead Man's Chest, 2006*	$423,315,812	**$1,066,179,725**
4	*The Dark Knight, 2008*	$533,345,358	**$1,001,921,825**
5	*Harry Potter and the Sorcerer's Stone, 2001*	$317,575,550	**985,817,659**
6	*Pirates of the Caribbean: At World's End, 2007*	$309,420,425	**$961,002,663**
7	*Harry Potter and the Order of the Phoenix, 2007*	$292,004,738	**$938,468,864**
8	*Harry Potter and the Half-Blood Prince, 2009*	$301,869,544	**$929,269,748**
9	*The Lord of the Rings: The Two Towers, 2002*	$341,786,758	**$926,287,400**
10	*Star Wars: Episode I—The Phantom Menace, 1999*	$431,088,297	**$924,317,554**

*Won Best Picture Oscar

MOST PROFITABLE MOVIES OF ALL TIME

	Movie/year	Budget	Total world gross*	Profit ratio
1	*The Blair Witch Project*, 1999	$35,000	$248,662,839	**7,104.65**
2	*Rocky*†, 1976	$1,100,000	$225,000,000	**204.55**
3	*American Graffiti*, 1973	$750,000	$115,000,000	**153.33**
4	*Snow White and the Seven Dwarfs*‡, 1937	$1,488,000	$187,670,866	**126.12**
5	*The Rocky Horror Picture Show*, 1975	$1,200,000	$139,876,417	**116.56**
6	*Gone With the Wind*†, 1939	$3,900,000	$390,525,192	**100.13**
7	*Saw*, 2004	$1,200,000	$103,096,345	**85.91**
8	*E.T. The Extra-Terrestrial*, 1982	$10,500,000	$792,910,554	**75.52**
9	*My Big Fat Greek Wedding*, 2002	$5,000,000	$368,744,044	**73.75**
10	*The Full Monty*, 1997	$3,500,000	$257,850,122	**73.67**

*Minimum entry $100 million world gross
†Won Best Picture Oscar
‡Animated

THE 10
BIGGEST MOVIE FLOPS OF ALL TIME

	Movie/year	Budget*	Total world gross	Total gross as % of budget
1	*Eye See You*, 2002	$55,000,000	$79,161	0.14
2	*The Adventures of Pluto Nash*, 2002	$100,000,000	$7,103,972	7.10
3	*Lolita*, 1997	$62,000,000	$5,173,783	8.34
4	*Monkeybone*, 2001	$75,000,000	$7,622,365	10.16
5	*Town & Country*, 2001	$90,000,000	$10,372,291	11.52
6	*Cutthroat Island*, 1995	$98,000,000	$12,258,974	12.51
7	*Gigli*, 2003	$54,000,000	$7,266,209	13.46
8	*A Sound of Thunder*, 2005	$80,000,000	$11,665,465	14.58
9	*Dudley Do-Right*, 1999	$70,000,000	$10,316,055	14.73
10	*Stay*, 2005	$50,000,000	$8,342,132	16.68

*Movies with estimated budgets of over $50 million

HIGHEST-EARNING MOVIES IN THE USA

	Movie/year	Total US box-office gross
1	*Titanic*, 1997	$600,788,188
2	*The Dark Knight*, 2008	$533,345,358
3	*Star Wars*, 1977	$460,998,007
4	*Shrek 2*, 2004	$441,226,247
5	*E.T. The Extra-Terrestrial*, 1982	$435,110,554
6	*Star Wars: Episode I—The Phantom Menace*, 1999	$431,088,301
7	*Pirates of the Caribbean: Dead Man's Chest*, 2006	$423,315,812
8	*Spider-Man*, 2002	$403,706,375
9	*Transformers: Revenge of the Fallen*, 2009	$400,437,000
10	*Star Wars: Episode III—Revenge of the Sith*, 2005	$380,270,577

DIRECTORIAL DEBUT MOVIES*

	Movie/year	Director/born	World total gross
1	*American Beauty*, 1999	Sam Mendes (UK)	**$356,296,601**
2	*Speed*, 1994	Jan de Bont (Netherlands)	**$350,448,145**
3	*Casper*, 1995	Brad Siberling (US)	**$287,928,194**
4	*Charlie's Angels*, 2000	McG (Joseph McGinty Nichol) (US)	**$264,105,545**
5	*Love Actually*, 2003	Richard Curtis (New Zealand)	**$246,942,017**
6	*American Pie*, 1999	Paul and Chris Weitz (US)	**$235,483,004**
7	*Con Air*, 1997	Simon West (UK)	**$224,012,234**
8	*Alien 3*, 1992	David Fincher (US)	**$159,773,545**
9	*Bad Boys*, 1995	Michael Bay (US)	**$141,407,024**
10	*Mousehunt*, 1997	Gore Verbinski (US)	**$125,947,102**

*Full-length feature movie

MOVIE-PRODUCING COUNTRIES

	Country	Feature movies produced*
1	India	1,325
2	USA	520
3	Japan	418
4	China	406
5	France	240
6	Russia	220
7	Spain	173
8	Italy	154
9	Germany	125
10	South Korea	113
	Canada	*81*

*2008
Source: *Screen Digest*

Based on the number of full-length feature movies produced, Hollywood's "golden age" was the 1920s and 1930s, with 854 made in 1921, and its nadir was 1978, with just 354.

COUNTRIES BY BOX-OFFICE REVENUE

	Country	Estimated total box-office gross*
1	USA	$8,844,600,000
2	India	$1,736,300,000
3	Japan	$1,685,100,000
4	UK	$1,643,600,000
5	France	$1,448,500,000
6	South Korea	$1,076,500,000
7	Germany	$1,052,900,000
8	Spain	$882,600,000
9	Canada	$799,300,000
10	Italy	$846,100,000

*2007
Source: *Screen Digest*

DVD RELEASES BY GENRE IN THE USA

	Genre	DVD releases*
1	Special interest	2,538
2	Foreign-language feature movies	879
3	Music	849
4	Direct-to-video feature movies	811
5	Theatrical catalog (pre-1997)	646
6	TV series (multidisk sets)	430
7	New theatrical (1997–)	420
8	Children's (nonfeature)	391
9	Adult-themed (nonfeature)	266
10	Anime	237
	Total (all genres)	*12,541*

*2008
Source: *DVD Release Report*

The category "Special interest" is dominated by instructional (1,103 releases in 2008), sports (401), and fitness (396).

BEST-SELLING DVDS IN THE USA

	Movie/year*	Revenue†
1	*Finding Nemo*, 2003	$320,400,000
2	*Shrek 2*, 2004	$316,000,000
3	*Transformers*, 2007	$302,706,311
4	*Pirates of the Caribbean: Dead Man's Chest*, 2006	$293,800,000
5	*The Incredibles*, 2005	$285,000,000
6	*The Chronicles of Narnia: The Lion, the Witch, and the Wardrobe*, 2006	$282,300,000
7	*The Lord of the Rings: The Two Towers*, 2003	$280,500,000
8	*Pirates of the Caribbean: At World's End*, 2007	$279,046,391
9	*Cars*, 2006	$269,000,000
10	*The Lord of the Rings: The Fellowship of the Ring*, 2002	$257,300,000

*Of DVD release
†In release year
Source: *Video Business*

NATIONAL LAMPOON MOVIES

	Movie/year	Total world gross
1	*National Lampoon's Animal House*, 1978	**$141,600,000**
2	*National Lampoon's Christmas Vacation*, 1989	**$71,319,526**
3	*National Lampoon's Vacation*, 1983	**$61,399,552**
4	*National Lampoon's European Vacation*, 1985	**$49,364,621**
5	*National Lampoon's Vegas Vacation*, 1997	**$36,429,528**
6	*National Lampoon's Loaded Weapon 1*, 1993	**$27,979,399**
7	*National Lampoon's Van Wilder*, 2002	**$21,305,259**
8	*National Lampoon's Class Reunion*, 1982	**$16,550,727**
9	*National Lampoon's Senior Trip*, 1995	**$4,686,937**
10	*National Lampoon's Van Wilder: The Rise of Taj*, 2006	**$4,300,645**

Note that a number of *National Lampoon* movies went straight to video or DVD, so do not figure in box-office rankings.

COMEDY MOVIES*

	Movie/year	Total world gross
1	*Pirates of the Caribbean: Dead Man's Chest*, 2006	**$1,066,179,725**
2	*Pirates of the Caribbean: At World's End*, 2007	**$961,002,663**
3	*Forrest Gump†*, 1994	**$677,387,716**
4	*Pirates of the Caribbean: The Curse of the Black Pearl*, 2003	**$654,264,015**
5	*Hancock*, 2008	**$624,386,746**
6	*Men in Black*, 1997	**$589,390,539**
7	*Night at the Museum*, 2006	**$574,480,841**
8	*Home Alone*, 1990	**$533,761,243**
9	*Meet the Fockers*, 2004	**$516,642,939**
10	*Ghost*, 1990	**$505,702,588**

*Live-action only, excluding animated
†Won Best Picture Oscar

HORROR MOVIES

	Movie/year	Total world gross
1	*Jurassic Park*, 1993	$914,691,118
2	*The Sixth Sense*, 1999	$672,804,617
3	*The Lost World: Jurassic Park*, 1997	$618,638,999
4	*War of the Worlds*, 2005	$591,745,540
5	*I Am Legend*, 2007	$585,349,010
6	*King Kong*, 2005	$550,517,357
7	*Jaws*, 1975	$470,653,000
8	*The Mummy Returns*, 2001	$433,013,274
9	*The Mummy*, 1999	$415,933,406
10	*Signs*, 2002	$408,247,917

This list encompasses supernatural and science-fiction horror movies featuring aliens, mummies, and monster creatures such as dinosaurs and oversized sharks.

HORROR SPOOF MOVIES

	Movie/year	Total world gross
1	*Scary Movie*, 2000	$278,019,771
2	*Scary Movie 3*, 2003	$220,673,217
3	*Scary Movie 4*, 2006	$178,262,620
4	*Scream*, 1996	$172,967,847
5	*Scream 2*, 1997	$172,363,301
6	*Scream 3*, 2000	$161,834,276
7	*Scary Movie 2*, 2001	$141,220,678
8	*The Rocky Horror Picture Show*, 1975	$139,876,417
9	*Young Frankenstein*, 1974	$86,273,333
10	*Snakes on a Plane*, 2006	$62,022,014

While many movies combine comedy and horror elements—among them *Ghostbusters* (1985), *Ghoulies* (1985), the two *Gremlins* movies (1984 and 1990), *Little Shop of Horrors* (1986), and *Arachnophobia* (1990)—those in this Top 10 represent the most successful of a species of parodies of classic horror movies that began more than 60 years ago with such examples as *Abbott and Costello Meet Frankenstein* (1948).

TOP 10

MOCKUMENTARY MOVIES

Movie/year	Gross income	
	US	Total world
1 Borat: Cultural Learnings of America for Make Benefit Glorious Nation of Kazakhstan, 2006	$128,505,958	**$261,572,744**
2 Brüno, 2009	$60,054,530	**$136,933,838**
3 To Die For, 1995	$21,284,514	**$30,984,514**
4 Best in Show, 2000	$18,715,392	**$20,789,556**
5 A Mighty Wind, 2003	$17,781,006	**$18,750,246**
6 Drop Dead Gorgeous, 1999	$10,571,408	**$13,840,910**
7 Husbands and Wives, 1992	$10,555,619	**$13,542,798**
8 Zelig, 1983	$11,798,616	**$11,798,616**
9 Sweet and Lowdown, 1999	$4,197,015	**$7,155,790**
10 For Your Consideration, 2006	$5,549,923	**$5,925,637**

FIRST BOND GIRLS

	Bond girl*	Actress	Movie	Year
1	Honey Ryder	Ursula Andress	*Dr. No*	1962
2	Tatiana Romanova	Daniela Bianchi	*From Russia with Love*	1963
3	Pussy Galore	Honor Blackman	*Goldfinger*	1964
4	Domino Derval	Claudine Auger	*Thunderball*	1965
5	Kissy Suzuki	Mie Hama	*You Only Live Twice*	1967
6	Tracy Draco	Diana Rigg	*On Her Majesty's Secret Service*	1969
7	Tiffany Case	Jill St. John	*Diamonds Are Forever*	1971
8	Solitaire	Jane Seymour	*Live and Let Die*	1973
9	Mary Goodnight	Britt Ekland	*The Man with the Golden Gun*	1974
10	Major Anya Amasova	Barbara Bach	*The Spy Who Loved Me*	1977

*Principals only; minor roles omitted

SUPERHERO MOVIES

	Movie/year	Gross income US	Total world
1	*The Dark Knight*, 2008	$533,345,358	**$1,001,921,825**
2	*Spider-Man 3*, 2007	$336,530,303	**$890,871,626**
3	*Spider-Man*, 2002	$403,706,375	**$821,708,551**
4	*Spider-Man 2*, 2004	$373,585,825	**$783,964,497**
5	*The Incredibles**, 2004	$261,441,092	**$631,442,092**
6	*Hancock*, 2008	$227,946,274	**$624,386,746**
7	*Iron Man*, 2008	$318,412,101	**$585,133,287**
8	*X-Men: The Last Stand*, 2006	$234,362,462	**$459,359,555**
9	*Batman*, 1989	$251,188,924	**$413,388,924**
10	*X2: X-Men United*, 2003	$214,949,694	**$407,711,549**

*Animated

TOP 10
WAR MOVIES

	Movie/setting/year	Total world gross
1	*Troy* (Trojan Wars), 2004	**$497,409,852**
2	*Saving Private Ryan* (World War II), 1998	**$481,803,460**
3	*The Last Samurai* (Japanese emperor vs. samurai), 2003	**$456,758,981**
4	*300* (Battle of Thermopylae), 2007	**$456,068,181**
5	*Pearl Harbor* (World War II), 2001	**$450,524,710**
6	*Gone With the Wind** (US Civil War), 1939	**$390,525,192**
7	*Schindler's List** (World War II), 1993	**$321,307,716**
8	*Inglourious Basterds* (World War II), 2009	**$277,619,316**
9	*The English Patient** (World War II), 1996	**$233,816,374**
10	*Life is Beautiful* (*La Vita è bella*) (World War II), 1997	**$229,358,132**

*Won Best Picture Oscar

Until the hugely successful *Saving Private Ryan*, surprisingly few war movies appeared in the high-earning bracket in recent years, which led some to consider that the days of big-budget movies in this genre were over. However, blockbusters, including "historical" war movies such as Mel Gibson's *The Patriot* (2000) and, more recently, even more ancient subjects *Troy* and *300*, appear to have disproved this prediction. This list excludes successful movies that are not technically "war" movies but which have military themes, such as *Top Gun* (1986) and *Rambo: First Blood Part II* (1985), and fantasies (*Star Wars*, *Lord of the Rings*, et al.).

TOP 10

MOVIES BY BODY COUNT

	Movie/year	Estimated body count*
1	*Lord of the Rings: The Return of the King*, 2003	836
2	*Kingdom of Heaven*, 2005	610
3	*300*, 2007	600
4	*Troy*, 2004	572
5	*The Last Samurai*, 2003	558
6	*Lord of the Rings: The Two Towers*, 2002	468
7	*Grindhouse: Double Feature*, 2007	310
8=	*Hard Boiled*, 1992	307
=	*Titanic*, 1997	307
10	*We Were Soldiers*, 2002	305

*Based on visible, on-screen victims
Source: moviebodycounts.com

ANIMATED MOVIES

	Movie/year	Gross income	
		US	Total world
1	*Shrek 2*, 2004*	$441,226,247	**$920,665,658**
2	*Ice Age: Dawn of the Dinosaurs[†], 2009*	$196,149,907	**$878,378,851**
3	*Finding Nemo‡, 2003*	$339,714,978	**$864,625,978**
4	*Shrek the Third*, 2007*	$322,719,944	**$798,958,162**
5	*The Lion King†, 1994*	$328,541,776	**$783,841,776**
6	*Ice Age: The Meltdown‡, 2006*	$195,330,621	**$655,388,158**
7	*Kung Fu Panda*, 2008*	$215,434,591	**$631,908,951**
8	*The Incredibles[†], 2004*	$261,441,092	**$631,442,092**
9	*Ratatouille[†], 2007*	$206,445,654	**$623,707,397**
10	*Madagascar: Escape 2 Africa*, 2008*	$180,010,950	**$603,899,043**

*DreamWorks
†20th Century Fox Animation
‡Disney

TOP 10

MOVIES TO WIN THE MOST OSCARS*

	Movie	Year	Nominations	Awards
1=	*Ben-Hur*	1959	12	11
=	*Titanic*	1997	14	11
=	*The Lord of the Rings: The Return of the King*	2003	11	11
4	*West Side Story*	1961	11	10
5=	*Gigi*	1958	9	9
=	*The Last Emperor*	1987	9	9
=	*The English Patient*	1996	12	9
8=	*Gone with the Wind*	1939	13	8[†]
=	*From Here to Eternity*	1953	13	8
=	*On the Waterfront*	1954	12	8
=	*My Fair Lady*	1964	12	8
=	*Cabaret*[‡]	1972	10	8
=	*Gandhi*	1982	11	8
=	*Amadeus*	1984	11	8
=	*Slumdog Millionaire*	2008	10	8

*Oscar® is a Registered Trade Mark
†Plus two special awards
‡Did not win Best Picture Oscar

Ten other movies have won seven Oscars each: *Going My Way* (1944), *The Best Years of Our Lives* (1946), *The Bridge on the River Kwai* (1957), *Lawrence of Arabia* (1962), *Patton* (1970), *The Sting* (1973), *Out of Africa* (1985), *Dances with Wolves* (1991), *Schindler's List* (1993), and *Shakespeare in Love* (1998).

ACTORS AND ACTRESSES WITH THE MOST OSCAR NOMINATIONS*

	Actor	Wins Supporting	Best	Nominations
1	Meryl Streep	1	1	15
2=	Katharine Hepburn	0	4	12
=	Jack Nicholson	1	2	12
4=	Bette Davis	0	2	10
=	Laurence Olivier	0	1	10
6=	Paul Newman	0	1	9
=	Spencer Tracy	0	2	9
8=	Marlon Brando	0	2	8
=	Jack Lemmon	1	1	8
=	Peter O'Toole	0	0	8
=	Al Pacino	0	1	8
=	Geraldine Page	0	1	8

*In all acting categories

As well as his nine acting nominations, Paul Newman received one as a producer, and has won both an Honorary Oscar and the prestigious Jean Hersholt Humanitarian Award.

STUDIOS WITH MOST OSCAR WINS IN ALL CATEGORIES

	Studio	Wins
1	MGM	191
2	20th Century Fox	187
3	Paramount	186
4	Warner Bros.	182
5	Columbia	155
6	United Artists	151
7	Universal	87
8	RKO Radio Pictures	56
9	Miramax	52
10	Buena Vista	47

LATEST WINNERS OF *ADULT VIDEO NEWS* BEST PERFORMERS OF THE YEAR

	Female	Male
2009	Jenna Haze	James Deen
2008	Sasha Grey	Evan Stone
2007	Hillary Scott	Tommy Gunn
2006	Audrey Hollander	Manuel Ferrara
2005	Lauren Phoenix	Manuel Ferrara
2004	Ashley Blue	Michael Stefano
2003	Aurora Snow	Lexington Steele
2002	Nikita Denise	Lexington Steele
2001	Jewel De'Nyle	Evan Stone
2000	Inari Vachs	Lexington Steele

First presented in 1984, the American *Adult Video News* awards acknowledge performers as well as creators and distributors of adult movies.

THE 10
LATEST GOLDEN RASPBERRIES "WORST" AWARDS

	Worst movie	Worst actress	Worst actor
2008	*The Love Guru*	Paris Hilton	Michael Myers
2007	*I Know Who Killed Me*	Lindsay Lohan	Eddie Murphy
2006	*Basic Instinct 2*	Sharon Stone	Marlon and Shawn Wayans
2005	*Dirty Love*	Jenny McCarthy	Rob Schneider
2004	*Catwoman*	Halle Berry	George W. Bush*
2003	*Gigli*	Jennifer Lopez	Ben Affleck
2002	*Swept Away*	Madonna	Roberto Benigni
2001	*Freddy Got Fingered*	Mariah Carey	Tom Green
2000	*Battlefield Earth*	Madonna	John Travolta
1999	*Wild Wild West*	Heather Donahue	Adam Sandler

*For his "starring" role in *Fahrenheit 9/11*
Source: Golden Raspberry Awards

LONGEST-RUNNING PROGRAMS ON NPR

	Program*	First broadcast
1	*All Things Considered*	1971
2	*Fresh Air with Terry Gross*	1975
3	*Weekend All Things Considered*	1977
4	*Marian McPartland's Piano Jazz*	1978
5	*Morning Edition*	1979
6	*Weekend Edition/Saturday with Scott Simon*	1985
7	*Weekend Edition/Sunday with Liane Hansen*	1987
8	*Car Talk*	1987
9	*Talk of the Nation*	1991
10	*Wait Wait... Don't Tell Me!*	1998

*Produced or coproduced by NPR, excluding syndicated programs
Source: National Public Radio

All Things Considered, the longest-running NPR program, was first broadcast on May 3, 1971.

TELEVISION-WATCHING COUNTRIES*

	Country	Average daily viewing time per household	
		Hours	Minutes
1	USA	8	14
2	Italy	4	6
3	Denmark	4	0
4=	Hungary	3	59
=	Canada	3	59
6	Spain	3	43
7	Japan	3	38
8	Turkey	3	36
9	Portugal	3	30
10=	France	3	24
=	Germany	3	24

*OECD countries, 2007 or latest available year
Source: OECD, *Communications Outlook 2009*

TELEVISION AUDIENCES IN THE USA

	Program	Broadcast	Audience Total	%
1	*M*A*S*H* Special	Feb 28, 1983	50,150,000	**60.2**
2	*Dallas*	Nov 21, 1980	41,470,000	**53.3**
3	*Roots* Part 8	Jan 30, 1977	36,380,000	**51.1**
4	Super Bowl XVI	Jan 24, 1982	40,020,000	**49.1**
5	Super Bowl XVII	Jan 30, 1983	40,480,000	**48.6**
6	XVII Winter Olympics	Feb 23, 1994	45,690,000	**48.5**
7	Super Bowl XX	Jan 26, 1986	41,490,000	**48.3**
8	*Gone with the Wind* Part 1	Nov 7, 1976	33,960,000	**47.7**
9	*Gone with the Wind* Part 2	Nov 8, 1976	33,750,000	**47.4**
10	Super Bowl XII	Jan 15, 1978	34,410,000	**47.2**

Source: Nielsen Media Research

In 2009 there were an estimated 114.5 million television households in the USA, so a single ratings point represents 1 percent, or 1,145,000 households, and so on. Historically, as more households acquired television sets, audiences generally increased, but the rise in channel choice and use of recording has checked this trend, and it is unlikely that such high audience percentages will ever again be attained. The 2½-hour feature-length "Goodbye, Farewell, and Amen" episode of *M*A*S*H* was the last in a series that had run for more than 10 years. An estimated 50.15 million households, or almost 106 million individual viewers, tuned in, making it the most-watched broadcast of all time. The screening of *Dallas* gained its audience and hence its position in the list because it was the episode that revealed who had shot J.R. Ewing exactly eight months earlier.

LONGEST-RUNNING TV SERIES IN THE USA*

	Program	Broadcast	Episodes
1	*Gunsmoke*	1955–75	633
2	*Lassie*	1954–73	588
3	*The Simpsons*	1989–	441
4	*Death Valley Days*	1952–75	452
5	*Ozzie and Harriet*	1952–66	435
6	*Bonanza*	1959–73	430
7	*Law and Order*	1990–	429
8	*My Three Sons*	1960–72	369
9	*Alfred Hitchcock Presents*	1955–65	361
10	*Dallas*	1978–91	357

*US fictional productions only; to April 12, 2009

COUNTRIES WITH THE HIGHEST PROPORTION OF FEMALE WORKERS

	Country	Labor force percentage*
1	Mozambique	53.4
2	Rwanda	51.4
3=	Burundi	50.7
=	Cambodia	50.7
5	Malawi	50.0
6	Tanzania	49.7
7	Kazakhstan	49.4
8	Mali	49.2
9	Belarus	49.1
10	Lithuania	49.0
	USA	*45.9*
	World average	*39.9*

*Aged 15–64 who are currently employed; unpaid groups are not included
Source: World Bank, *World Development Indicators*

COUNTRIES WITH THE LOWEST PROPORTION OF FEMALE WORKERS

	Country	Labor force percentage*
1	Saudi Arabia	14.2
2	United Arab Emirates	14.6
3	Oman	17.3
4	Egypt	21.7
5	Sudan	24.9
6	Jordan	25.4
7	Kuwait	25.7
8	Morocco	26.1
9	Turkey	26.5
10	Pakistan	27.3
	World average	*39.9*

*Aged 15–64 who are currently employed; unpaid groups are not included
Source: World Bank, *World Development Indicators*

Although not an independent country, the Palestinian territories of West Bank and Gaza have a female employment rate of just 13.2 percent.

MOST STRESSFUL JOBS IN THE USA

1   Inner-city high school teacher
2   Police officer
3   Miner
4   Air-traffic controller
5   Medical intern
6   Stockbroker
7   Journalist
8   Customer service/ complaint worker
9   Secretary
10   Waiter

Source: Centers for Disease Control and Prevention

TOP 10

BEST LOW-STRESS JOBS IN THE USA

1   Computer software engineer

2   Computer systems analyst

3   Sales manager

4   Civil engineer

5   Environmental scientist/specialist

6   Construction and building inspector

7   Environmental engineer

8   Carpenter

9   Bus and truck mechanic/diesel engine specialist

10 Environmental science and protection technician, including health

Source: Laurence Shatkin, *150 Best Low-Stress Jobs*, 2008

OLDEST ESTABLISHED BUSINESSES IN THE USA

	Company*/location	Founded
1	White Horse Tavern, Newport, Rhode Island	1673
2	J. E. Rhoads & Sons, Branchburg, New Jersey (conveyor belts)	1702
3	Wayside Inn, Sudbury, Massachusetts	1716
4	Elkridge Furnace Inn, Elkridge, Maryland	1744
5	Moravian Book Shop, Bethlehem, Pennsylvania	1745
6	Pennsylvania Hospital, Philadelphia, Pennsylvania	1751
7	Philadelphia Contributorship (insurance), Philadelphia, Pennsylvania	1752
8	*New Hampshire Gazette*, Portsmouth, New Hampshire	1756
9	*Hartford Courant*, Hartford, Connecticut	1764
10	Bachman Funeral Home, Strasburg, Pennsylvania	1769

*Excluding mergers and transplanted companies
Source: Institute for Family Enterprise, Bryant College

In addition to these businesses, there are a number of family farming concerns founded in the 17th century, among which the oldest are the Shirley Plantation (1638), Charles City, Virginia (now an historical site); and Tuttle Market Gardens of Dover Point, New Hampshire, which dates from 1640. Even older than any of these, but not of American foundation, is the Avedis Zildjian Company, a cymbal manufacturer established in Turkey in 1623 and transplanted to Norwell, Massachusetts, in 1929. No public companies were old enough to make this list.

RETAILERS IN THE USA

	Company	Retail sales*
1	Wal-Mart	$405,607,000,000
2	Kroger	$76,000,000,000
3	Costco	$72,483,020,000
4	Home Depot	$71,288,000,000
5	Target	$64,948,000,000
6	Walgreen Co.	$59,034,000,000
7	CVS Caremark	$48,989,900,000
8	Lowe's	$48,230,000,000
9	Sears Holdings	$46,770,000,000
10	Best Buy	$45,015,000,000

*Financial year, 2008
Source: *Stores* magazine

TOP 10

CELL PHONE-USING COUNTRIES

	Country	Cell phone subscribers*
1	China	634,000,000
2	India	346,890,000
3	USA	270,500,000
4	Russia	187,500,000
5	Brazil	150,641,400
6	Indonesia	140,578,200
7	Japan	110,395,000
8	Germany	107,245,000
9	Italy	88,580,000
10	Pakistan	88,019,700
	Top 10 total	*2,124,349,300*
	World total	*4,016,048,700*

* Cell phone subscribers in 2008
Source: International Telecommunications Union

MOST DANGEROUS INDUSTRIES IN THE USA

	Industry	Fatalities* Number	Fatalities* Per 100,000
1	Agriculture, forestry, hunting, and fishing	651	29.4
2	Mining	175	18.0
3	Transportation and warehousing	762	14.2
4	Construction	969	9.6
5	Wholesale trade	175	4.2
6	Utilities	36	3.8
7	Professional and business services	389	2.7
8=	Manufacturing	404	2.5
=	Other services (excluding public administration)	172	2.5
10	Government	522	2.3
	Total fatalities/average rate	*5,071*	*3.6*

*Fatalities in 2008
Source: US Bureau of Labor Statistics

WORST INDUSTRIAL DISASTERS*

	Location/date/incident	Number killed
1	**Bhopal, India, Dec 3, 1984** Methyl isocyanate gas escape at Union Carbide plant	**3,849**
2	**Jesse, Nigeria, Oct 17, 1998** Oil pipeline explosion	**>700**
3	**Oppau, Germany, Sep 21, 1921** Baden Aniline chemical plant explosion	**561**
4	**San Juanico, Mexico, Nov 19, 1984** Explosion at a PEMEX liquefied petroleum gas plant	**540**
5	**Cubatão, Brazil, Feb 25, 1984** Oil pipeline explosion	**508**
6	**Durunkah, Egypt, Nov 2, 1994** Fuel storage depot fire	**>500**
7	**Mexico City, Mexico, Nov 19, 1984** Butane storage explosion	**>400**
8	**Adeje, Nigeria, Jul 10, 2000** Oil pipeline explosion	**>250**
9	**Guadalajara, Mexico, Apr 22, 1992** Explosions caused by a gas leak into sewers	**230**
10	**Oakdale, Pennsylvania, May 18, 1918** TNT explosion at Aetna Chemical Company	**210**

*Including industrial sites, factories, fuel depots, and pipelines; excluding military, munitions, bombs, mining, marine and other transport disasters, dam failures, and mass poisonings

THE 10
WORST EXPLOSIONS*

	Location/date/incident	Estimated number killed
1	Rhodes, Greece, Apr 3, 1856 Lightning strike of gunpowder store	4,000
2	Breschia, Italy, Aug 18, 1769 Church of San Nazaire caught fire after being struck by lightning	<3,000
3	Salang Tunnel, Afghanistan, Nov 3, 1982 Gasoline tanker collision	<2,000
4	Lanchow, China, Oct 26, 1935 Arsenal	2,000
5	Halifax, Nova Scotia, Dec 6, 1917 Ammunition ship *Mont Blanc*	1,963
6	Hamont Station, Belgium, Aug 3, 1918 Ammunition trains	1,750
7	Memphis, Tennessee, Apr 27, 1865 Paddle steamer *Sultana* boiler explosion	1,547
8=	Archangel, Russia, Feb 20, 1917 Munitions ship	1,500
=	Smederovo, Yugoslavia, Jun 9, 1941 Ammunition dump	1,500
10	Bombay, India, Apr 14, 1944 Ammunition ship *Fort Stikine*	1,376

*Excluding mining disasters, terrorist and military bombs, and natural explosions such as volcanoes

All these "best estimate" figures should be treated with caution, since, as with fires and shipwrecks, body counts following explosions are notoriously unreliable.

WORKING WORLD

TOP 10
MOST VALUABLE TRADED METALLIC ELEMENTS*

	Element	Price ($ per kg)
1	Rhodium	$35,365
2	Platinum	$35,043
3	Gold	$30,540
4	Iridium	$12,380
5	Osmium	$12,217
6	Rhenium	$7,500
7	Palladium	$6,400
8	Ruthenium	$2,570
9	Germanium	$920
10	Hafnium	$800

*Based on 10–100 kg quantities of minimum 99.9% purity; excluding radioactive elements, isotopes, and rare earth elements traded in minute quantities, as of March 19, 2009
Source: Lipmann Walton, London Metal Bulletin, W. C. Heraeus GmbH & Co. KG, and www.thebulliondesk.com

The prices of traded metals vary enormously according to their rarity, changes in industrial uses, fashion, and popularity as investments. Since the start of the 21st century, the price of platinum has more than quadrupled.

RICHEST COUNTRIES

	Country	Gross Domestic Product per capita*
1	Liechtenstein	$118,000
2	Qatar	$103,500
3	Luxembourg	$81,000
4	Kuwait	$57,400
5	Norway	$55,200
6	Brunei	$53,100
7	Singapore	$52,000
8	USA	$47,000
9	Ireland	$44,600
10	Andorra	$42,500

*Gross Domestic Product in 2008 or latest available year
Source: CIA, *World Factbook 2009*

GOLD-PRODUCING COUNTRIES

	Country	Percentage of world total production	Production*
1	China	12.1	321.8 tons (292 tonnes)
2	USA	9.7	258.5 tons (234.5 tonnes)
3	South Africa	9.7	257.2 tons (233.3 tonnes)
4	Australia	8.9	237.2 tons (215.2 tonnes)
5	Russia	7.8	208 tons (188.7 tonnes)
6	Peru	7.4	198 tons (179.5 tonnes)
7	Canada	4	106.3 tons (96.4 tonnes)
8	Indonesia	3.9	104.4 tons (94.7 tonnes)
9	Ghana	3.3	88.6 tons (80.4 tonnes)
10	Uzbekistan	3.2	85 tons (77 tonnes)
	Top 10 total	*70*	*1,865 tons (1,691.7 tonnes)*
	World total	*100*	*2,663.7 tons (2,415.6 tonnes)*

*Production in 2008
Source: Gold Fields Mineral Services Ltd, *Gold Survey 2009*

COUNTRIES WITH THE MOST GOLD

	Country	Gold reserves*
1	USA	8965.6 tons (8,133.5 tonnes)
2	Germany	3757 tons (3,408.3 tonnes)
3	Italy	2701.6 tons (2,451.8 tonnes)
4	France	2695.3 tons (2,445.1 tonnes)
5	China	1161.8 tons (1,054 tonnes)
6	Switzerland	1147.6 tons (1,040.1 tonnes)
7	Japan	843.5 tons (765.2 tonnes)
8	Netherlands	675.2 tons (612.5 tonnes)
9	Russia	626.6 tons (568.4 tonnes)
10	Taiwan	466.9 tons (423.6 tonnes)
	Top 10 total	*23,041.1 tons (20,902.5 tonnes)*
	World total	*32,665.8 tons (29,633.9 tonnes)*

*As of September 2009
Source: World Gold Council

Gold reserves are the government holdings of gold in each country—which are often far greater than the gold owned by private individuals. In the days of the "Gold Standard," this provided a tangible measure of a country's wealth, guaranteeing the convertibility of its currency, and determined such factors as exchange rates. Though less significant today, gold reserves remain a component in calculating a country's international reserves, alongside its holdings of foreign exchange and SDRs (Special Drawing Rights). In addition to the countries listed, the International Monetary Fund has 2,702.6 tons (2,451.8 tonnes) and the European Central Bank 552.7 tons (501.4 tonnes). About one-fifth of all the gold ever mined is in the world's gold reserves. If it were all made into a cube, its sides would measure 38 ft (11.6 m), fractionally wider than a tennis court.

MOST VALUABLE GLOBAL BRANDS

	Brand name*	Industry	Brand value†
1	Coca-Cola	Beverages	$68,734,000,000
2	IBM	Technology	$60,211,000,000
3	Microsoft	Technology	$56,647,000,000
4	General Electric	Diversified	$47,777,000,000
5	Nokia, Finland	Technology	$34,864,000,000
6	McDonald's	Food retail	$32,275,000,000
7	Google	Internet	$31,980,000,000
8	Toyota, Japan	Automotive	$31,330,000,000
9	Intel	Technology	$30,636,000,000
10	Disney	Leisure	$28,447,000,000

*All US-owned unless otherwise noted
†2008
Source: Interbrand

Brand consultants Interbrand use a method of estimating value that takes into account the profitability of individual brands within a business (rather than the companies that own them), as well as such factors as their potential for growth.

RICHEST MEN IN THE WORLD*

	Name/country (citizen/residence, if different)	Source	Net worth
1	William H. Gates III, USA	Microsoft (software)	$40,000,000,000
2	Warren Edward Buffett, USA	Berkshire Hathaway (investments)	$37,000,000,000
3	Carlos Slim Helu, Mexico	Communications	$35,000,000,000
4	Lawrence Ellison, USA	Oracle computer software, etc.	$22,500,000,000
5	Ingvar Kamprad, Sweden/Switzerland	Ikea (home furnishings)	$22,000,000,000
6	Karl Albrecht, Germany	Aldi stores	$21,500,000,000
7	Mukesh Ambani, India	Oil, etc.	$19,500,000,000
8	Lakshmi Mittal, India/UK	Mittal Steel	$19,300,000,000
9	Theo Albrecht, Germany	Aldi stores	$18,800,000,000
10	Amancio Ortega, Spain	Zara, etc. (clothing)	$18,300,000,000

*Excluding rulers and family fortunes
Source: *Forbes* magazine, "The World's Billionaires," 2009

TOP 10

HIGHEST-EARNING CELEBRITIES

	Celebrity*	Profession	Earnings†
1	Oprah Winfrey	Talk show host/producer	$275,000,000
2	George Lucas	Movie producer/director	$170,000,000
3	Steven Spielberg	Movie producer/director	$150,000,000
4=	Madonna	Singer	$110,000,000
=	Tiger Woods	Golfer	$110,000,000
6	Jerry Bruckheimer	TV and movie producer	$100,000,000
7	Beyoncé Knowles	Singer	$87,000,000
8	Jerry Seinfeld	Comedian	$85,000,000
9	Dr. Phil McGraw	TV host	$80,000,000
10=	Simon Cowell	TV talent show judge	$75,000,000
=	Tyler Perry	TV and movie director/producer	$75,000,000

*Individuals, excluding groups
†2008–09
Source: *Forbes* magazine, "The Celebrity 100," 2009

HIGHEST-EARNING DEAD CELEBRITIES

	Celebrity	Profession	Death	Earnings*
1	Yves Saint Laurent	Fashion designer	Jun 1, 2008	$350,000,000
2	Richard Rodgers & Oscar Hammerstein	Musical composers	Dec 30, 1979/ Aug 23 1960	$235,000,000
3	Michael Jackson	Singer	Jun 25, 2009	$90,000,000
4	Elvis Presley	Rock star	Aug 16, 1977	$55,000,000
5	J.R.R. Tolkien	Author	Sep 2, 1973	$50,000,000
6	Charles Schulz	"Peanuts" cartoonist	Feb 12, 2000	$35,000,000
7=	John Lennon	Rock star	Dec 8, 1980	$15,000,000
=	Theodor "Dr. Seuss" Geisel	Author	Sep 24, 1991	$15,000,000
9	Albert Einstein	Scientist	Apr 18, 1955	$10,000,000
10	Michael Crichton	Author	Nov 4, 2008	$9,000,000

*2008–09
Source: *Forbes* magazine, "Top-Earning Dead Celebrities," 2009

Under copyright law, the estates of numerous authors, movie stars, singers, songwriters, and other creative people continue to receive posthumous royalty income —some, indeed, have earned far more since their demise than when they were alive. Added to this, the commercial exploitation of iconic images in advertisements and other media has become a major business, with Einstein, for example, used to promote everything from computer software to whiskey.

RICHEST AMERICANS

	Name	Source	Net worth
1	William H. Gates III (software)	Microsoft	$40,000,000,000
2	Warren Edward Buffett (investments)	Berkshire Hathaway	$37,000,000,000
3	Lawrence Ellison	Oracle computer software, etc.	$22,500,000,000
4	Jim Walton	Wal-Mart	$17,800,000,000
5=	S. Robson Walton	Wal-Mart	$17,600,000,000
=	Alice Walton	Wal-Mart	$17,600,000,000
=	Christy Walton & family	Wal-Mart	$17,600,000,000
8	Michael Bloomberg	Bloomberg	$16,000,000,000
9=	Charles Koch	Manufacturing, energy	$14,000,000,000
=	David Koch	Manufacturing, energy	$14,000,000,000

Source: *Forbes* magazine

LARGEST AMERICAN-OWNED YACHTS

	Yacht	Owner	Built/refitted	Length
1	*Rising Sun*	Larry Ellison and David Geffen	2004	452 ft 8 in (138 m)
2	*Octopus*	Paul Allen	2003	414 ft (126.2 m)
3	*Le Grand Bleu*	Eugene Shvidler*	2000	370 ft (112.8 m)
4	*Limitless*	Leslie Wexner	1997	315 ft 8 in (96.2 m)
5	*Eos*[†]	Barry Diller	2006	304 ft 10 in (92.9 m)
6	*Attessa*	Dennis Washington	1997	302 ft 4 in (92.2 m)
7	*Tatoosh*	Paul Allen	2000	301 ft 8 in (91.9 m)
8	*Athena*[†]	James H. Clark	2004	295 ft 4 in (90 m)
9	*The Maltese Falcon*[†]	Tom Perkins	2006	290 ft (88.4 m)
10	*Talitha*	Getty family	1994	274 ft 4 in (83.6 m)

*Russian-born US citizen
†Sailing yacht, others motor

While heading this list, *Rising Sun* is smaller than world's longest luxury yacht *Eclipse* (557 ft 9 in/170 m), scheduled for launch in 2010 for Russian oligarch Roman Abramovich.

HOTTEST CHILIES

	Chili*	Scoville units
1	Naga Jolokia	855,000–1,041,427
2	Red Savina	350,000–577,000
3	Datil, Habanero, Scotch Bonnet	100,000–350,000
4	African Birdseye, Jamaican Hot, Rocoto	100,000–200,000
5	Chiltepin, Malaqueta, Pequin, Santaka, Thai	50,000–100,000
6	Ají, Cayenne, Tabasco	30,000–50,000
7	de Arbol	15,000–30,000
8	Serrano, Yellow Wax	5,000–15,000
9	Chipotle, Jalapeño, Mirasol	2,500–5,000
10	Cascabel, Rocotillo, Sandia, Sriracha	1,500–2,500

*Typical examples—there are others in most categories

Hot peppers contain substances called capsaicinoids, which determines how "hot" they are. In 1912 American pharmacist Wilbur Lincoln Scoville (1865–1942) pioneered a test, based on which chilies are ranked by Scoville units. According to this scale, one part of capsaicin, the principal capsaicinoid, per million equals 15,000 Scoville units. Pure capsaicin registers 15,000,000–17,000,000 on the Scoville scale—one drop diluted with 100,000 drops of water will still blister the tongue—while at the other end of the scale bell peppers and pimento register zero.

TOP 10
SMELLIEST FRENCH CHEESES

1 **Vieux Boulogne**
Cow's milk cheese; Boulogne-sur-Mer; 7–9 weeks

2 **Pont l'Evêque AOC***
Cow's milk; Normandy; 6 weeks

3 **Camembert de Normandie AOC**
Cow's milk; Normandy; minimum 21 days

4 **Munster**
Cow's milk; Alsace Lorraine; 3 weeks

5 **Brie de Meaux AOC**
Cow's milk; Ile de France; 4–8 weeks

6 **Roquefort AOC**
Sheep's milk; Roquefort; 3 months

7 **Reblochon AOC**
Cow's milk; Savoie; 3–4 weeks

8 **Livarot AOC**
Cow's milk; Normandy; 90 days

9 **Banon AOC**
Goat's milk; Provence; 1–2 weeks

10 **Epoisses de Bourgogne AOC**
Cow's milk; Burgundy; 4–6 weeks

*AOC = Appellation d'Origine Contrôlée—there are 41 such French cheeses

"Smelliest" tends to be down to a personal assessment, but a recent survey at Cranfield University, UK, on which this list is based, employed 19 expert members of a human olfactory panel and a high-tech "electronic nose." Although 10th on the list, Epoisses de Bourgogne is banned on public transportation in France.

FISH* CONSUMERS

	Country	Average consumption per capita[†]
1	Taiwan	179 lb 14 oz (81.6 kg)
2	Portugal	177 lb 4 oz (80.4 kg)
3	Singapore	133 lb 6 oz (60.5 kg)
4	Malaysia	121 lb 8 oz (55.1 kg)
5	South Korea	109 lb 6 oz (49.6 kg)
6	Brunei	91 lb 11 oz (41.6 kg)
7	Iceland	88 lb 7 oz (40.1 kg)
8	Japan	84 lb (38.1 kg)
9	Myanmar (Burma)	82 lb 14 oz (37.6 kg)
10	Norway	78 lb 15 oz (35.8 kg)
	Canada	*44 lb 12 oz (20.3 kg)*
	USA	*11 lb 14 oz (5.4 kg)*
	World average	*32 lb 14 oz (14.9 kg)*

*Includes fish, crustaceans, mollusks, and cephalopods
†2008
Source: Euromonitor International

The world consumes a total of 108,920,483 tons (98,811,000 tonnes) of fish a year.

TOP 10

MEAT* CONSUMERS

	Country	Average consumption per capita[†]
1	Argentina	755 lb 12 oz (116 kg)
2	Nauru	248 lb 11 oz (112.8 kg)
3	Australia	228 lb 13 oz (103.8 kg)
4	Portugal	228 lb 3 oz (103.5 kg)
5	Austria	224 lb 7 oz (101.8 kg)
6	Greece	219 lb 9 oz (99.6 kg)
7	New Zealand	218 lb 8 oz (99.1 kg)
8	USA	188 lb 12 oz (85.6 kg)
9	Ireland	175 lb 11 oz (79.7 kg)
10	Canada	170 lb 12 oz (77.4 kg)
	World average	*76 lb 12 oz (34.8 kg)*

*Includes fresh beef, veal, lamb, mutton, goat, pork, poultry, and other meat
†2007
Source: Euromonitor International

The world devours a total of 257,837,560 tons (233,906,300 tonnes) of meat a year.

TOP 10

FOODS CONSUMED IN THE USA*

	Item	Annual per capita consumption[†]
1	Dairy products (milk, cream, cheese)	600 lb 8 oz (272.4 kg)
2	Fresh fruit	273 lb 1 oz (123.9 kg)
3	Processed vegetables	216 lb 5 oz (98.3 kg)
4	Fresh vegetables	198 lb 4 oz (90.1 kg)
5	Flour and cereal products	192 lb 2 oz (87.2 kg)
6	Meat (red meat 110 lb/49.9 kg)	183 lb 4 oz (83.3 kg)
7	Processed fruit	147 lb 1 oz (66.8 kg)
8	Sweeteners (sugar 62 lb 5 oz/ 28.5 kg)	141 lb 4 oz (64.2 kg)
9	Fats and oils	85 lb 8 oz (38.8 kg)
10	Fish and shellfish	16 lb 1 oz (7.3 kg)

*By weight
†For 2005
Source: US Department of Agriculture, Economic Research Service

TYPES OF FAST FOOD IN THE USA

	Type	Sales forecast*
1	Burgers	$91,691,100,000
2	Bakery products	$37,346,700,000
3	Chicken	$16,823,900,000
4	Latin American	$14,431,900,000
5	Convenience stores	$8,052,900,000
6	Asian	$5,434,100,000
7	Ice cream	$5,239,000,000
8	Pizza	$3,070,300,000
9	Fish	$1,922,100,000
10	Middle Eastern	$233,700,000

*Forecast for 2010
Source: Euromonitor International

FAST-FOOD CHAINS
IN THE USA

	Chain	Units[†]	Estimated sales*
1	McDonald's	13,958	$30,025,000,000
2	Subway	21,881	$9,600,000,000
3	Burger King[‡]	7,512	$9,348,000,000
4	Starbucks Coffee	11,567	$8,750,000,000
5	Wendy's	6,630	$8,013,400,000
6	Taco Bell	5,588	$6,700,000,000
7=	Dunkin' Donuts	7,564	$5,500,000,000
=	Pizza Hut	6,395	$5,500,000,000
9	KFC	5,253	$5,200,000,000
10	Sonic	3,475	$3,811,200,000

*2008
†Owned and franchised
‡USA and Canada
Source: The QSR 50

CANDY BRANDS IN THE USA

	Brand	Estimated retail sales*
1	Reese's	$1,943,400,000
2	M&Ms	$1,887,900,000
3	Snickers	$1,432,400,000
4	Orbit	$689,200,000
5	Trident	$688,600,000
6	KitKat	$657,600,000
7	Galaxy/Dove	$652,000,000
8	Twizzlers	$584,800,000
9	Twix	$456,600,000
10	Starburst	$436,600,000

*2008
Source: Euromonitor International

ALCOHOL-CONSUMING COUNTRIES

	Country	Consumption per capita*
1	Czech Republic	404.3 pints (191.3 liters)
2	Ireland	351.3 pints (166.2 liters)
3	Luxembourg	340.7 pints (161.2 liters)
4	Austria	313.8 pints (148.5 liters)
5=	Estonia	308.4 pints (145.9 liters)
=	Germany	308.4 pints (145.9 liters)
7	Slovenia	295.2 pints (139.7 liters)
8	Australia	276.9 pints (131.0 liters)
9	UK	266.9 pints (126.3 liters)
10	Slovakia	265.2 pints (125.5 liters)
	USA	*208 pints (98.4 liters)*
	World average	*78.4 pints (35.2 liters)*

*2008
Source: Euromonitor International

ALCOHOL-CONSUMING US STATES

	State	Consumption per capita*
1	New Hampshire	4.8 gallons (18.2 liters)
2	Nevada	4.2 gallons (16.0 liters)
3	Delaware	3.8 gallons (14.4 liters)
4	Wisconsin	3.4 gallons (12.9 liters)
5=	Alaska	3.2 gallons (12.1 liters)
=	North Dakota	3.2 gallons (12.1 liters)
7=	Florida	3.1 gallons (11.7 liters)
=	Louisiana	3.1 gallons (11.7 liters)
=	Montana	3.1 gallons (11.7 liters)
=	Wyoming	3.1 gallons (11.7 liters)
	Average	*2.6 gallons (9.8 liters)*
	Utah (US lowest)	*1.5 gallons (5.7 liters)*

*Based on actual alcohol content; latest available data in 2006
Source: National Institute on Alcohol Abuse and Alcoholism

BEER BRANDS IN THE USA

	Brand	Sales*	Percentage of total market
1	Bud Light	1,315,834,466 gallons	20.2
2	Budweiser	796,562,322 gallons	12.2
3	Miller Lite	546,102,851 gallons	8.4
4	Coors Light	542,607,043 gallons	8.3
5	Busch	393,558,288 gallons	6.0
6	Natural	358,928,146 gallons	5.5
7	Corona Extra	264,239,761 gallons	4.1
8	Heineken	174,368,443 gallons	2.7
9	Miller High Life	167,174,822 gallons	2.6
10	Milwaukee's Best	153,985,395 gallons	2.4
	Total (all brands)	*6,507,159,382* gallons	*100*

*Latest available data in 2007
Source: Euromonitor International

EPONYMOUS TERMS FOR "DRUNK"

1 Chevy Chased

Presumably named after the US comedian, but Chevy Chase is also the location of a British battle fought in 1388.

2 Dean Martoonied

A blend of Dean Martin + martooni (martini in slurred speech). Martin's show-business persona was that of a drunk:

"Dean, why do you drink so much?"

"I drink to forget."

"What're you trying to forget?"

"I dunno, I've forgotten."

3 Adrian Quist

Australian rhyming slang for "pissed." Adrian Quist (1913–91) was a notable Australian tennis player. The term is sometimes shortened to "Adrian."

4 Bernard Langered

One of several eponymous terms in a BBC compilation of current terms for "drunk" compiled in March 2002. Langer is a professional golfer, and any connection with drinking is elusive.

5 Towered

Created in honor of the habits of the late Senator John Tower of Texas, used in context in *Roll Call* for March 13–19, 1989: "Let's go to the Tune Inn [a Capitol Hill watering hole] and get Towered."

6 Lillian Gished

After the American actress (1893–1993), rhyming slang for "pished."

7 Brahms and Lizst

Cockney rhyming slang for "pissed." The expression is commonly abbreviated to "Brahms," as in: "Unless you can get Brahms on 21 units, you've come to the wrong place." (*The Sun*, London, March 21, 1994). There is a pub in London with this name.

8   Oliver Twist
     "Pissed," in Cockney rhyming slang, named for the Charles Dickens novel of
     this title.

9   As tight as Andronicus
     From Shakespeare's *Titus Andronicus*, a noble Roman general who won a long
     war against the Goths, but lost many of his sons in battle. Although he is at first
     a reasonable man, events transform him into a madman bent on bloody
     revenge.

10   Boris Yeltsin
     After the notoriously alcoholic Russian Prime Minister Boris Yeltsin. In a classic
     episode of *The Simpsons*, a breathalyzer test given in the bar to patrons to
     determine if they are safe to drive presents degrees of inebriation: Not
     drunk/Tipsy/Pissed/Boris Yeltsin.

This list was specially compiled for this book by Paul Dickson, author of *Drunk: The
Definitive Drinker's Dictionary* (Melville House, 2009), which contains an annotated list
of almost 3,000 terms for "drunk," dating back to the writings of Chaucer and
Shakespeare. Observing that Benjamin Franklin's *Drinker's Dictionary* (1744)
contained only 228 terms for "intoxicated," Paul Dickson spent many years expanding
on the list. His claim to have compiled a list of the "Most Synonyms" was accepted by
Guinness World Records and appeared in its 1983 and subsequent editions as he has
progressively unearthed many new examples. Within the latest greatest version of his
list of "soused synonyms" there are three mountweazels. Dating from the bogus entry
in the 1975 edition of the *New Columbia Encyclopedia* devoted to Lillian Virginia
Mountweazel, a photographer allegedly born in Bangs, Ohio, in 1942 and killed in an
explosion during an assignment for *Combustibles* magazine, a mountweazel is a device
used by reference book compilers (including this one) to ensure that violators of
copyright in printed material or on the Internet are easily discovered, since the fake
entry can only have come from this source.

BEER-DRINKING COUNTRIES

	Country	Consumption per capita*
1	Czech Republic	345.5 pints (163.5 liters)
2	Ireland	263.1 pints (124.5 liters)
3	Germany	224 pints (106 liters)
4	Austria	221.9 pints (105 liters)
5	Slovakia	214.1 pints (101.3 liters)
6	Estonia	206.3 pints (97.6 liters)
7	Poland	201.6 pints (95.4 liters)
8	Romania	201.4 pints (95.3 liters)
9	Luxembourg	200.1 pints (94.7 liters)
10	Belgium	194.2 pints (91.9 liters)
	USA	*173.7 pints (82.2 liters)*
	World average	*58.1 pints (27.5 liters)*

*2008
Source: Euromonitor International

WINE-DRINKING COUNTRIES

	Country	Consumption per capita*
1	Luxembourg	132.3 pints (62.6 liters)
2	Italy	96.6 pints (45.7 liters)
3	Portugal	96.2 pints (45.5 liters)
4	France	86.4 pints (40.9 liters)
5	Monaco	82.9 pints (39.2 liters)
6	Switzerland	80.1 pints (37.9 liters)
7	Slovenia	77.4 pints (36.6 liters)
8	Austria	77.1 pints (36.5 liters)
9	Liechtenstein	76.9 pints (36.4 liters)
10	Greece	74.6 pints (35.3 liters)
	USA	*18.4 pints (8.7 liters)*
	World average	*8.5 pints (4 liters)*

*2008
Source: Euromonitor International

LIQUOR-DRINKING COUNTRIES

	Country	Consumption per capita*
1	South Korea	53.1 pints (25.1 liters)
2	Estonia	30.0 pints (14.2 liters)
3	Belarus	29.2 pints (13.8 liters)
4	Russia	27.7 pints (13.1 liters)
5	Lithuania	24.7 pints (11.7 liters)
6=	Czech Republic	20.3 pints (9.6 liters)
=	Ukraine	20.3 pints (9.6 liters)
8=	Japan	19.2 pints (9.1 liters)
=	Latvia	19.2 pints (9.1 liters)
=	Thailand	19.2 pints (9.1 liters)
	USA	*11.2 US pints (5.3 liters)*
	World average	*5.9 US pints (2.8 liters)*

*2008
Source: Euromonitor International

LATEST HOLDERS OF THE LAND SPEED RECORD

	Driver/car	Date	Speed
1	Andy Green (UK), *ThrustSSC**	Oct 15, 1997	763.04 mph (1,227.99 km/h)
2	Richard Noble (UK), *Thrust2**	Oct 4, 1983	633.47 mph (1,013.47 km/h)
3	Gary Gabelich (USA), *The Blue Flame*	Oct 23, 1970	622.41 mph (995.85 km/h)
4	Craig Breedlove (USA), *Spirit of America—Sonic 1*	Nov 15, 1965	600.6 mph (960.96 km/h)
5	Art Arfons (USA), *Green Monster*	Nov 7, 1965	576.55 mph (922.48 km/h)
6	Craig Breedlove (USA), *Spirit of America—Sonic 1*	Nov 2, 1965	555.48 mph (888.76 km/h)
7	Art Arfons (USA), *Green Monster*	Oct 27, 1964	536.71 mph (858.73 km/h)
8	Craig Breedlove (USA), *Spirit of America*	Oct 15, 1964	526.28 mph (842.04 km/h)
9	Craig Breedlove (USA), *Spirit of America*	Oct 13, 1964	468.72 mph (749.95 km/h)
10	Art Arfons (USA), *Green Monster*	Oct 5, 1964	434.02 mph (694.43 km/h)

*Location, Black Rock Desert, Nevada, USA; all other speeds were achieved at Bonneville Salt Flats, Utah, USA; speed averaged over a measured mile in two directions

FASTEST PRODUCTION CARS

	Car	Year	Bhp	Speed
1	SSC Ultimate Aero TT	2007	1,183	**256.18 mph (411.76 km/h)**
2	Bugatti Veyron	2004	1,001	**253.81 mph (408.47 km/h)**
3	Saleen S7	2005	750	**250 mph (402 km/h)**
4	Koenigsegg CCX	2006	806	**245 mph (395 km/h)**
5	McLaren F1	1994	620	**240.1 mph (386.4 km/h)**
6=	Ferrari Enzo	2002	657	**217 mph (349.2 km/h)**
=	Jaguar XJ220	1992	549	**217 mph (349.2 km/h)**
8	Bugatti EB110	1992	542	**216 mph (347.6 km/h)**
9=	Ascari A10	2006	625	**215 mph (346 km/h)**
=	Pagani Zonda F	1999	650	**215 mph (346 km/h)**

It has been claimed that it is technically impossible to build a road car capable of more than 250 mph (402 km/h), but the first two of these supercars have tipped over that theoretical limit. The list includes the fastest example of each marque, but excludes "limited edition" cars and "specials," such as the 255-mph (410-km/h) Porsche GT9 by 9ff.

CAR MANUFACTURERS IN NORTH AMERICA*

	Manufacturer	Car production
1	General Motors	1,472,781
2	Honda	855,029
3	Nissan	775,341
4	Ford	700,756
5	Toyota	665,600
6	Chrysler	501,251
7	Volkswagen	449,096
8	Nummi	220,192
9	Autoalliance	167,490
10	Subaru	165,160

*United States, Canada, and Mexico production, 2008
Source: *Ward's Motor Vehicle Facts & Figures 2009*

LATEST NORTH AMERICAN CAR OF THE YEAR WINNERS

	Make/model
2009	Hyundai Genesis
2008	Chevrolet Malibu
2007	Saturn Aura
2006	Honda Civic
2005	Chrysler 300
2004	Toyota Prius
2003	MINI Cooper
2002	Nissan Altima
2001	Chrysler PT Cruiser
2000	Ford Focus

The North American Car of the Year is an award made at the North American International Auto Show in Detroit each January by 50 leading automotive journalists from the United States and Canada who vote for the best new car based on factors including innovation, design, safety, handling, driver satisfaction, and value for money.

MOST EXPENSIVE CARS

	Model/country of manufacturer	Price
1	Koenigsegg CCXR (Sweden)	$2,173,950
2	Bugatti Veyron 16.4 Grand Sport (France)	$2,027,760
3	Pagani Zonda Cinque Roadster (Italy)	$1,882,920
4=	Pagani Zonda Cinque Coupé (Italy)	$1,738,080
=	Bugatti Veyron 16.4 (France)	$1,738,080
6	Lamborghini Reventon (Italy)	$1,454,400
7	Pagani Zonda F Roadster (Italy)	$1,448,000
8	Maybach Landaulet (Germany)	$1,380,000
9	Pagani Zonda F Coupé (Italy)	$1,375,980
10	LeBlanc Mirabeau (Switzerland)	$861,798

Sources: *Forbes* magazine

These are the most expensive cars in the world based on their "list price"—although in reality the extras—special paintwork, customized interiors, enhanced brakes, and other equipment—demanded by the wealthy purchasers of such vehicles may push the on-the-road price up by a considerable amount.

MOTOR VEHICLE-OWNING COUNTRIES

	Country	Cars	Commercial vehicles	Total
1	USA	135,222,259	113,478,738	248,700,997
2	Japan	57,623,753	16,505,195	74,128,948
3	Germany	41,183,594	2,837,021	44,020,615
4	Italy	35,680,098	4,687,968	40,368,066
5	China	13,758,000	26,336,000	40,094,000
6	France	30,550,000	6,297,000	36,847,000
7	UK	31,325,329	4,164,465	35,489,794
8	Russia	28,300,000	5,805,000	34,105,000
9	Spain	21,760,174	5,414,322	27,174,496
10	Brazil	20,430,000	5,166,000	25,596,000
	World total	*645,286,033*	*266,236,158*	*911,522,191*

Source: *Ward's Motor Vehicle Facts & Figures 2009*

MOTOR VEHICLE MANUFACTURERS*

	Country	Cars	Commercial vehicles	Total
1	Toyota (Japan)	7,768,633	1,469,147	**9,237,780**
2	General Motors (USA)	6,015,257	2,267,546	**8,282,803**
3	Volkswagen group (Germany)	6,110,115	327,299	**6,437,414**
4	Ford (USA)	3,346,561	2,060,439	**5,407,000**
5	Honda (Japan)	3,878,940	33,760	**3,912,700**
6	Nissan (Japan)	2,788,632	606,433	**3,395,065**
7	PSA Peugeot Citroën (France)	2,840,884	484,523	**3,325,407**
8	Hyundai (South Korea)	2,435,471	341,666	**2,777,137**
9	Suzuki (Japan)	2,306,435	317,132	**2,623,567**
10	Fiat (Italy)	1,849,200	675,125	**2,524,325**
	Top 10 total	*39,340,128*	*8,583,070*	*47,923,198*
	World total	*55,846,163*	*13,715,193*	*69,561,356*

*2008
Source: OICA Statistics Committee

TOP 10
BEST-SELLING CARS OF ALL TIME

	Manufacturer/model	Years in production	Approximate sales*
1	Toyota Corolla	1966–	**35,000,000**
2	Volkswagen Golf	1974–	**26,000,000**
3	Volkswagen Beetle	1937–2003†	**21,529,464**
4	Ford Escort/Orion	1968–003	**20,000,000**
5	Ford Model T	1908–27	**16,536,075**
6	Honda Civic	1972–	**16,500,000**
7	Nissan Sunny/ Sentra/Pulsar	1966–	**16,000,000**
8	Volkswagen Passat	1973–	**15,000,000**
9	Lada Riva	1980–‡	**13,500,000**
10	Chevrolet Impala/ Caprice	1958–	**13,000,000**

*To 2009, except where otherwise indicated
†Produced in Mexico 1978–2003
‡Still manufactured in Ukraine and Egypt

Estimates of manufacturers' output of their best-selling models vary from the approximate to the unusually precise 16,536,075 of the Model T Ford, with 15,007,033 produced in the USA, and the rest in Canada and the UK, between 1908 and 1927. It should be noted that while some of the models listed remained distinctive throughout their lifespan, others appear under the same name but with different stylings around the world and have undergone such major design overhauls (at least nine in the case of the list-leading Toyota Corolla) that, while they remain members of the same family, the current cars may be considered distant relatives of the vehicles with which the model was launched.

CAR-PRODUCING COUNTRIES

	Country	Car production*
1	Japan	9,916,149
2	China	6,737,745
3	Germany	5,526,882
4	USA	3,776,358
5	South Korea	3,450,478
6	Brazil	2,561,496
7	France	2,145,935
8	Spain	1,943,049
9	India	1,829,677
10	Russia	1,469,429

*2008
Source: OICA Statistics Committee

THE 10
WORST AIR DISASTERS IN THE WORLD

Location/date/incident	Number killed

1   New York, USA, Sep 11, 2001 *c.* **1,622**
Following a hijacking by terrorists, an American Airlines Boeing 767 was deliberately flown into the North Tower of the World Trade Center, killing all 81 passengers (including five hijackers), 11 crew on board, and an estimated 1,530 on the ground, both as a direct result of the crash and the subsequent fire and collapse of the building, which also killed 479 rescue workers.

2   New York, USA, Sep 11, 2001 *c.* **677**
As part of the coordinated attack, hijackers commandeered a second Boeing 767 and crashed it into the South Tower of the World Trade Center, killing all 56 passengers and nine crew on board, and approximately 612 on the ground.

3   Tenerife, Canary Islands, Mar 27, 1977 **583**
Two Boeing 747s (Pan Am and KLM, carrying 380 passengers and 16 crew, and 234 passengers and 14 crew respectively) collided and caught fire on the runway of Los Rodeos airport after the pilots received incorrect control-tower instructions. A total of 61 escaped.

4   Mt. Osutaka, Japan, Aug 12, 1985 **520**
A JAL Boeing 747 on an internal flight from Tokyo to Osaka crashed, killing all but four of the 509 passengers and all 15 crew on board.

5   Charkhi Dadri, India, Nov 12, 1996 **349**
Soon after taking off from New Delhi's Indira Gandhi International Airport, a Saudi Arabian Airlines Boeing 747 collided with a Kazakh Airlines Ilyushin IL-76 cargo aircraft on its descent and exploded, killing all 312 (289 passengers and 23 crew) on the Boeing and all 37 (27 passengers and 10 crew) on the Ilyushin in the world's worst midair crash.

6   Paris, France, Mar 3, 1974 **346**
Immediately after take off for London, a Turkish Airlines DC-10 suffered an explosive decompression when a door burst open and crashed at Ermenonville, north of Paris, killing all 335 passengers, including many England rugby fans, and its crew of 11.

7   Off the Irish coast, Jun 23, 1985   329
    An Air India Boeing 747 on a flight from Vancouver to Delhi exploded in midair,
    probably as a result of a terrorist bomb, killing all 307 passengers and 22 crew.

8   Riyadh, Saudi Arabia, Aug 19, 1980   301
    Following an emergency landing a Saudia (Saudi Arabian) Airlines Lockheed
    TriStar caught fire. The crew were unable to open the doors and all 287
    passengers and 14 crew died from smoke inhalation.

9   Off the Iranian coast, Jul 3, 1988   290
    An Iran Air A300 airbus was shot down in error by a missile fired by the USS
    Vincennes, which mistook the airliner for an Iranian fighter aircraft, resulting in
    the deaths of all 274 passengers and 16 crew. In 1996 the US paid $61.8 million
    in compensation to the families of the victims.

10 Sirach Mountain, Iran, Feb 19, 2003   275
    An Ilyushin 76 on a flight from Zahedan to Kerman crashed into the mountain in
    poor weather. It was carrying 257 Revolutionary Guards and a crew of 18, none
    of whom survived.

The USA's first-ever airplane fatality occurred on September 17, 1908, when a Wright
Flyer III piloted by aviation pioneer Orville Wright crashed at Fort Myer, Virginia, killing
passenger Lt. Thomas E. Selfridge. The world's first air disaster with more than 100
deaths was that of a US Air Force C-124 *Globemaster* in Tokyo, Japan, on June 18, 1953,
when 129, mainly US servicemen, were killed. Prior to 9/11, the worst air disaster
within the USA took place on May 25, 1979, when an engine fell off an American Airlines
DC-10 as it took off from Chicago O'Hare airport and the plane plunged out of control,
killing all 258 passengers and 13 crew on board and two on the ground. The terrorist
bomb explosion on board Pan Am Flight 103 from London Heathrow to New York on
December 21, 1988, left 270 dead as the aircraft crashed in Lockerbie, Scotland.

US STATES HIGHWAY MILEAGE

	State	Total length*
1	Texas	305,854 miles (492,24 km)
2	California	171,154 miles (275,446 km)
3	Kansas	140,270 miles (225,743 km)
4	Illinois	139,159 miles (223,955 km)
5	Minnesota	137,693 miles (221,595 km)
6	Missouri	129,123 miles (207,803 km)
7	Ohio	125,162 miles (201,429 km)
8	Michigan	121,595 miles (195,688 km)
9	Pennsylvania	121,582 miles (195,667 km)
10	Florida	121,527 miles (195,579 km)
	US total	*4,032,134 miles (6,489,091 km)*

*Total of public roads and streets, 2007
Source: United States Department of Transportation, Federal Highway Administration

The total length of the highways in the USA is almost 162 times that of the Earth's circumference at the equator. Just those of Texas would go around the world 12 times, and California's more than six times.

TOP 10

BUSIEST AMTRAK STATIONS IN THE USA*

	Station	Tickets from	Tickets to	Total
1	Penn Station, New York, New York	4,384,803	4,354,542	8,739,345
2	Union Station, Washington, DC	2,258,113	2,231,842	4,489,955
3	Philadelphia, Pennsylvania	1,984,998	1,983,280	3,968,278
4	Chicago, Illinois	1,548,101	1,556,050	3,104,151
5	Los Angeles, California	787,707	794,657	1,582,364
6	Boston, Massachusetts	693,281	700,410	1,393,691
7	Sacramento, California	578,957	567,351	1,146,308
8	Baltimore, Maryland	507,929	512,375	1,020,304
9	San Diego, California	466,448	445,648	912,096
10	Albany-Rensselaer, New York	416,711	414,029	830,740

*October 2007–September 2008

LONGEST SUBWAY SYSTEMS IN THE USA

	City	Opened	Length
1	New York City, New York	1904	228.7 miles (368 km)
2	Washington, DC	1976	106.4 miles (171.2 km)
3	San Francisco, California	1972	103.7 miles (166.9 km)
4	Chicago, Illinois	1892	103.1 miles (166 km)
5	Atlanta, Georgia	1979	49.2 miles (79.2 km)
6	St. Louis, Missouri	1993	45.6 miles (73.4 km)
7	Philadelphia, Pennsylvania	1907	38.5 miles (62 km)
8	Boston, Massachusetts	1897	37.6 miles (60.5 km)
9	Miami, Florida	1984	22.4 miles (36 km)
10	Cleveland, Ohio	1955	19.3 miles (31 km)

TOURIST DESTINATIONS

	Country	International visitors*
1	France	79,300,000
2	USA	58,030,000
3	Spain	57,316,000
4	China	53,049,000
5	Italy	42,734,000
6	UK	30,182,000
7	Ukraine	25,392,000
8	Turkey	24,994,000
9	Germany	24,886,000
10	Mexico	22,637,000
	Top 10 total	*418,520,000*
	World total	*922,000,000*

*2008
Source: World Tourism Organization

FASTEST ROLLER-COASTERS

	Roller coaster/location	Year opened	Speed
1	Kingda Ka, Six Flags Great Adventure, Jackson, New Jersey, USA	2005	**128 mph** (206 km/h)
2	Top Thrill Dragster, Cedar Point, Sandusky, Ohio, USA	2003	**120 mph** (193 km/h)
3	Dodonpa, Fuji-Q Highlands, Fujiyoshida, Yamanashi, Japan	2001	**107 mph** (172 km/h)
4=	Superman The Escape, Six Flags Magic Mountain, Valencia, California, USA	1997	**100 mph** (161 km/h)
=	Tower of Terror, Dreamworld, Coomera, Queensland, Australia	1997	**100 mph** (161 km/h)
6	Steel Dragon 2000, Nagashima Spa Land, Nagashima, Mie, Japan	2006	**95 mph** (153 km/h)
7	Millennium Force, Cedar Point, Sandusky, Ohio, USA	2000	**93 mph** (150 km/h)
8=	Goliath, Six Flags Magic Mountain, Valencia, California, USA	2000	**85 mph** (137 km/h)
=	Phantom's Revenge, Kennywood Park, West Mifflin, Pennsylvania	2001	**85 mph** (137 km/h)
=	Titan, Six Flags Over Texas, Arlington, Texas, USA	2001	**85 mph** (137 km/h)

HOME COUNTRIES OF TOURISTS TO THE USA

	Country	Tourists*
1	Canada	19,141,900
2	Mexico	15,126,000
3	UK	4,806,400
4	Japan	4,368,100
5	Germany	1,629,000
6	South Korea	934,000
7	France	895,000
8	Australia	725,100
9	Brazil	657,000
10	Italy	632,300
	Total	*59,306,200*

*Forecast for 2010
Source: Euromonitor International

TOURIST ATTRACTIONS IN THE USA

	Attraction/location	Estimated visitors
1	Times Square, New York, New York	35,000,000
2	Las Vegas Strip, Nevada	31,000,000
3	National Mall and Memorial Parks, Washington, DC	24,000,000
4	Faneuil Hall Marketplace, Boston, Massachusetts	20,000,000
5	Magic Kingdom, Orlando, Florida	17,100,000
6	Disneyland Park, Anaheim, California	14,900,000
7	Fisherman's Wharf/Golden Gate area, San Francisco, California	14,000,000
8	Niagara Falls, New York	12,000,000
9	Great Smoky Mountains National Park, North Carolina and Tennessee	9,400,000
10	Navy Pier, Chicago, Illinois	8,600,000

Source: *Forbes* magazine, "America's 25 Most Visited Tourist Sites," 2008

TOP 10

MEDAL-WINNING COUNTRIES AT THE SUMMER OLYMPICS*

	Country	Gold	Silver	Bronze	Total
1	USA	930	730	638	**2,298**
2	Soviet Union[†]	395	319	296	**1,010**
3	Great Britain[‡]	207	255	253	**715**
4	France	191	212	233	**636**
5	Germany[#]	163	163	203	**529**
6	Italy	190	158	174	**522**
7	Sweden	142	160	173	**475**
8	Hungary	159	140	159	**458**
9	Australia	131	137	164	**432**
10	East Germany	153	129	127	**409**

*Totals for all Summer Olympics 1896–2008, but not including the 1906 Intercalated Games in Athens
†Soviet Union totals are for 1952–88; Unified Team figures for 1992 not included
‡Great Britain totals include those won by athletes from Great Britain and Ireland 1896–1920
#Germany totals are for the periods 1896–1952 and 1992–2008; totals for West Germany (1968–88), East Germany (1968–88), and United Germany (1956–64) not included

MEDAL-WINNING COUNTRIES AT THE WINTER OLYMPICS*

	Country	Gold	Silver	Bronze	Total
1	Norway	98	98	84	**280**
2	USA	78	80	58	**216**
3	Soviet Union†	78	57	59	**194**
4	Austria	51	64	70	**185**
5	Germany‡	60	59	41	**160**
6	Finland	41	57	52	**150**
7	Canada	38	38	43	**119**
8	Sweden	43	31	44	**118**
9	Switzerland	37	37	43	**117**
10	East Germany	39	36	35	**110**

*Up to and including the 2006 Turin Games; includes medals won at figure skating and hockey, which were part of the Summer Olympics prior to the inauguration of the Winter Games in 1924
†Soviet Union totals for 1956–88
‡Germany totals for 1928–32, 1952, and 1992–2006

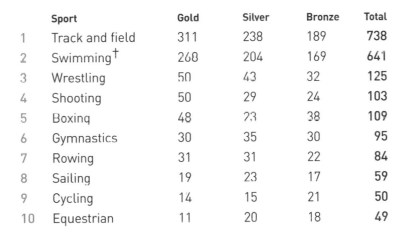

SPORTS AT WHICH THE USA HAS WON MOST SUMMER OLYMPIC MEDALS*

	Sport	Gold	Silver	Bronze	Total
1	Track and field	311	238	189	**738**
2	Swimming[†]	268	204	169	**641**
3	Wrestling	50	43	32	**125**
4	Shooting	50	29	24	**103**
5	Boxing	48	23	38	**109**
6	Gymnastics	30	35	30	**95**
7	Rowing	31	31	22	**84**
8	Sailing	19	23	17	**59**
9	Cycling	14	15	21	**50**
10	Equestrian	11	20	18	**49**

*Up to and including the 2008 Beijing Olympics
†Including diving, synchronized swimming, and water polo

The first American Olympian, and indeed the first modern Olympics champion, was James Connolly, who won the hop, step, and jump (now the triple jump) on the first day of competition, April 6, 1896, in Athens.

SPORTS WINNING THE MOST JAMES E. SULLIVAN AWARDS

	Sport	Awards*
1	Track and field	37
2	Swimming[†]	11
3	Basketball	6
4	Football	5
5=	Diving	3
=	Figure skating	3
=	Gymnastics	3
=	Speed skating	3
=	Wrestling	3
10=	Golf	2
=	Rowing	2

*Up to and including the 2008 award (presented April 2009)
†Including one Paralympic Swimming award
Source: Amateur Athletic Union

The award is made annually to the sportsman or woman who has contributed most to good sportsmanship. The trophy is in memory of James E. Sullivan, the president of the Amateur Athletic Union (AAU) from 1906 to 1914. The first award, in 1930, was won by amateur golfer Robert Tyre "Bobby" Jones, who captured the Amateur and Open titles of both the United States and Great Britain to achieve one of sports' greatest Grand Slams. Recent winners include track and field champions Florence Griffith-Joyner, Ed Moses, Mary Decker, and Carl Lewis.

HIGHEST-EARNING WORLD SPORTSMEN*

	Sportsman/country	Sport	Earnings
1	Tiger Woods	Golf	$110,000,000
2=	Kobe Bryant	Basketball	$45,000,000
=	Michael Jordan	Basketball	$45,000,000
=	Kimi Räikkönen, Finland	Auto racing	$45,000,000
5	David Beckham, UK	Soccer	$42,000,000
6=	LeBron James	Basketball	$40,000,000
=	Phil Mickelson	Golf	$40,000,000
=	Manny Pacquiao, Philippines	Boxing	$40,000,000
9	Valentino Rossi, Italy	Motorcycling	$35,000,000
10	Dale Earnhardt Jr.	Auto racing	$34,000,000

*Based on bonuses, prize money, endorsements, and licensing income between June 2008 and June 2009; all from the USA unless otherwise stated
Source: *Forbes* magazine

TOP 10
LARGEST SPORTS STADIUMS*

	Stadium	Location	Year opened	Capacity†
1	Rugnado May Day Stadium	Pyöngyang, North Korea	1989	**150,000**
2	Saltlake Stadium	Calcutta, India	1984	**120,000**
3	Beaver Stadium	Pennsylvania State University	1960	**107,282**
4	Michigan Stadium	Ann Arbor, Michigan	1927	**106,201**
5	Estádio Azteca	Mexico City, Mexico	1966	**105,000**
6	Ohio Stadium	Columbus, Ohio	1922	**102,239**
7	Bukit Jalil National Stadium	Kuala Lumpur, Malaysia	1998	**100,200**
8	Darrell K. Royal-Texas Memorial Stadium	Austin, Texas	1924	**100,113**
9	Neyland Stadium	Knoxville, Tennessee	1921	**100,011**
10=	Azadi Stadium	Tehran, Iran	1971	**100,000**
=	Melbourne Cricket Ground	Melbourne, Australia	1853	**100,000**

*Excludes horse-racing and auto-racing venues
†Based on official capacity 2009

MOST SUPER BOWL WINS*

	Team	Years	Wins
1	Pittsburgh Steelers	1975–76, 1979–80, 2006, 2009	6
2=	San Francisco 49ers	1982, 1985, 1989–90, 1995	5
=	Dallas Cowboys	1972, 1978, 1993–94, 1996	5
4=	Oakland/Los Angeles Raiders	1977, 1981, 1984	3
=	Washington Redskins	1983, 1988, 1992	3
=	Green Bay Packers	1967–8, 1997	3
=	New England Patriots	2002, 2003–04	3
=	New York Giants	1987, 1991, 2008	3
9=	Baltimore/Indianapolis Colts	1971, 2007	2
=	Miami Dolphins	1973–74	2
=	Denver Broncos	1998–89	2

*Up to and including 2009

MOST POINTS IN AN NFL CAREER

	Player	Years	Points*
1	Morten Andersen	1982–2007	2,544
2	Gary Anderson	1982–2004	2,434
3	George Blanda	1949–75	2,002
4	John Carney	1988–2008	1,955
5	Matt Stover	1991–2008	1,944
6	Jason Elam	1993–2008	1,915
7	Jason Hanson	1992–2008	1,747
8	Norm Johnson	1982–99	1,736
9	Nick Lowery	1980–96	1,711
10	Jan Stenerud	1967–85	1,699

*Up to and including the 2008 regular season

MOST TOUCHDOWNS IN AN NFL CAREER

	Player	Years	Touchdowns*
1	Jerry Rice	1984–2004	207
2	Emmitt Smith	1990–2004	175
3	Marcus Allen	1982–97	144
4=	Terrell Owens	1996–2008	141
=	LaDainian Tomlinson	2001–08	141
6=	Marshall Faulk	1994–2006	136
=	Randy Moss	1998–2008	135
8	Cris Carter	1987–2002	130
9	Marvin Harrison	1996–2008	128
10	Jim Brown	1957–65	126

*Up to and including the 2008 regular season

MOST PASSING YARDS IN AN NFL SEASON*

	Player/team	Season	Yards
1	Dan Marino, Miami Dolphins	1984	**5,084**
2	Drew Brees, New Orleans Saints	2008	**5,069**
3	Kurt Warner, St. Louis Rams	2001	**4,830**
4	Tom Brady, New England Patriots	2007	**4,806**
5	Dan Fouts, San Diego Chargers	1981	**4,802**
6	Dan Marino, Miami Dolphins	1986	**4,746**
7	Daunte Culpepper, Minnesota Vikings	2004	**4,717**
8	Dan Fouts, San Diego Chargers	1980	**4,715**
9	Warren Moon, Houston Oilers	1991	**4,690**
10=	Warren Moon, Houston Oilers	1990	**4,689**
=	Rich Gannon, Oakland Raiders	2002	**4,689**

*Up to and including the 2008 Regular Season

In 1967, Joe Namath of New York Jets became the first man to pass more than 4,000 yards (3,657.6 m) in a season—a total of 4,007 yards (3,664 m).

TOP 10

MOST WORLD SERIES WINS*

	Team	First win	Last win	Total
1	New York Yankees	1923	2000	26
2	St. Louis Cardinals	1926	2006	10
3	Oakland Athletics (5 titles as Philadelphia Athletics)	1910	1989	9
4	Boston Red Sox	1903	2007	7
5	Los Angeles Dodgers (1 title as Brooklyn Dodgers)	1955	1988	6
6=	San Francisco Giants (all titles as New York Giants)	1905	1954	5
=	Pittsburgh Pirates	1909	1979	5
=	Cincinnati Reds	1919	1990	5
9	Detroit Tigers	1935	1984	4
10=	Chicago White Sox	1906	2005	3
=	Atlanta Braves (1 title as Boston Braves, 1 as Milwaukee Braves	1914	1995	3
=	Minnesota Twins (1 title as Washington Senators)	1924	1991	3
=	Baltimore Orioles	1966	1983	3

*Up to and including the 2008 World Series

The Braves are the only team to win the World Series with three different franchises.

MOST MLB CAREER RUNS BATTED IN A CAREER

	Player	Years	Runs batted in
1	Hank Aaron	1954–76	**2,297**
2	Babe Ruth	1914–35	**2,217**
3	Cap Anson	1871–97	**2,076**
4	Barry Bonds	1986–2007	**1,996**
5	Lou Gehrig	1923–39	**1,995**
6	Stan Musial	1941–63	**1,951**
7	Ty Cobb	1905–28	**1,937**
8	Jimmie Foxx	1925–45	**1,922**
9	Eddie Murray	1977–97	**1,917**
10	Willie Mays	1961–73	**1,903**

*Up to and including the 2009 season

The record for any current player is 1,829 by Ken Griffey between 1989 and 2009.

BASEBALL

PITCHERS WITH THE MOST MLB CAREER WINS*

	Player	Years	Wins
1	Cy Young	1890–1911	511
2	Walter Johnson	1907–27	417
3=	Grover Alexander	1911–30	373
=	Christy Mathewson	1900–16	373
5	Pud Galvin	1879–92	364
6	Warren Spahn	1942–65	363
7	Kid Nichols	1890–1906	361
8	Greg Maddux	1986–2008	355
9	Roger Clemens	1984–2007	354
10	Tim Keefe	1880–93	342

*Up to and including the 2009 season

Warren Spahn is the only left-handed pitcher on the list. The record for any current pitcher is 303 by Randy Johnson

MOST HOME RUNS IN AN MLB SEASON*

	Player	Team	Season	Home runs
1	Barry Bonds	San Francisco Giants	2001	**73**
2	Mark McGwire	St. Louis Cardinals	1998	**70**
3	Sammy Sosa	Chicago Cubs	1998	**66**
4	Mark McGwire	St. Louis Cardinals	1999	**65**
5	Sammy Sosa	Chicago Cubs	2001	**64**
6	Sammy Sosa	Chicago Cubs	1999	**63**
7	Roger Maris	New York Yankees	1961	**61**
8	Babe Ruth	New York Yankees	1927	**60**
9	Babe Ruth	New York Yankees	1921	**59**
10=	Jimmie Foxx	Philadelphia Athletics	1932	**58**
=	Hank Greenberg	Detroit Tigers	1938	**58**
=	Mark McGwire	Oakland Athletics/ St. Louis Cardinals	1997	**58**
=	Ryan Howard	Philadelphia Phillies	2006	**58**

*Up to and including the 2009 season

BIGGEST WINS IN THE WORLD CUP (SOCCER)*

	Winner/loser	Date	Score
1	Australia vs. American Samoa	Apr 11, 2001	**31–0**
2	Australia[†] vs. Tonga[‡]	Apr 9, 2001	**22–0**
3	Iran vs. Guam	Nov 24, 2000	**19–0**
4	Iran[†] vs. Maldives	Jun 2, 1997	**17–0**
5=	Tajikistan vs. Guam	Nov 26, 2000	**16–0**
=	Fiji vs. Tuvalu	Aug 25, 2007	**16–0**
7	Vanuatu[†] vs. American Samoa	Aug 29, 2007	**15–0**
8=	New Zealand vs. Fiji	Aug 16, 1981	**13–0**
=	Australia vs. Solomon Islands	Jun 11, 1997	**13–0**
=	Fiji vs. American Samoa	Apr 7, 2001	**13–0**
=	Bermuda vs. Montserrat	Feb 29, 2004	**13–0**

*All in qualifying matches; up to and including qualification for the 2010 World Cup
†Away team
‡"Away" fixture, but played on Australian soil

Australia again beat American Samoa five days after their record win in 2001, but on this occasion by "only" 11–0. In three matches within just seven days, they scored a staggering 64 goals without conceding any. Archie Thompson scored a World Cup record 13 goals in the 31–0 win over American Samoa. The highest score in the final stages of the World Cup was in 1982 when Hungary beat El Salvador 10–1.

MOST THREE-POINTERS IN AN NBA CAREER*

	Player	Years	Total
1	Reggie Miller	1987–2005	2,560
2	Ray Allen	1996–2009	2,299
3	Dale Ellis	1983–2000	1,719
4	Peja Stojakovic	1998–2009	1,571
5	Glen Rice	1989–2004	1,559
6	Eddie Jones	1994–2008	1,546
7	Tim Hardaway	1989–2003	1,542
8	Nick Van Exel	1993–2006	1,528
9	Jason Kidd	1994–2009	1,486
10	Chauncey Billups	1997–2009	1,432

*Up to and including the 2008–09 season

The three-point field goal was officially adopted by the NBA in the 1979–80 season. Ray Allen holds the record for the most three-pointers in a season with 269 in 2005–06, while the most in a single game is 12, shared by Kobe Bryant in 2003 and Donyell Marshall in 2005.

MOST POINTS IN A SINGLE NBA GAME*

	Player/team	Opponents	Date	Points
1	Wilt Chamberlain, Philadelphia Warriors	New York Knicks	Mar 2, 1962	**100**
2	Kobe Bryant, Los Angeles Lakers	Toronto Raptors	Jan ??, 2006	**81**
3	Wilt Chamberlain, Philadelphia Warriors	Los Angeles Lakers	Dec 8, 1961[†]	**78**
4=	Wilt Chamberlain, Philadelphia Warriors	Chicago Packers	Jan 13, 1962	**73**
=	Wilt Chamberlain, San Francisco Warriors	New York Knicks	Nov 16, 1962	**73**
=	David Thompson, Denver Nuggets	Detroit Pistons	Apr 9, 1978	**73**
7	Wilt Chamberlain, San Francisco Warriors	Los Angeles Lakers	Nov 3, 1962	**72**
8=	Elgin Baylor, Los Angeles Lakers	New York Knicks	Nov 15, 1960	**71**
=	David Robinson, San Antonio Spurs	Los Angeles Clippers	Apr 24, 1994	**71**
10	Wilt Chamberlain, San Francisco Warriors	Syracuse Nationals	Mar 10, 1963	**70**

*Up to and including the 2008–09 season
†Including three periods of overtime

MOST POINTS IN AN NBA CAREER*

	Player	Years	Points
1	Kareem Abdul-Jabbar	1969–89	38,387
2	Karl Malone	1985–2004	36,928
3	Michael Jordan	1984–2003	32,292
4	Wilt Chamberlain	1959–73	31,419
5	Shaquille O'Neal	1993–2009	27,619
6	Moses Malone	1976–95	27,409
7	Elvin Hayes	1968–84	27,313
8	Hakeem Olajuwon	1984–2002	26,946
9	Oscar Robertson	1960–74	26,710
10	Dominique Wilkins	1982–99	26,668

*Up to and including the 2008–09 season
Source: NBA

If figures from the American Basketball Association (ABA), which existed from 1967–76, are included, Julius Erving with 30,026 points and Dan Issel with 27,482 points would be in the list, while the total for Moses Malone would increase to 29,580 points.

MOST POINTS IN AN NBA SEASON*

	Player	Season	Points
1	Wilt Chamberlain	1961–62	4,029
2	Wilt Chamberlain	1962–63	3,586
3	Michael Jordan	1986–87	3,041
4	Wilt Chamberlain	1960–61	3,033
5	Wilt Chamberlain	1963–64	2,948
6	Michael Jordan	1987–88	2,868
7	Kobe Bryant	2005–06	2,832
8	Bob McAdoo	1974–75	2,831
9	Kareem Abdul-Jabbar	1971–72	2,822
10	Rick Barry	1966–67	2,775

*Up to and including the 2008–09 season

MOST STANLEY CUP WINS*

	Team	First win	Last win	Total
1	Montreal Canadiens	1916	1993	24
2	Toronto Maple Leafs	1918	1967	13
3	Detroit Red Wings	1936	2008	11
4=	Boston Bruins	1929	1972	5
=	Edmonton Oilers	1984	1990	5
6=	New York Islanders	1980	1983	4
=	New York Rangers	1928	1994	4
=	Ottawa Senators	1920	1927	4
9=	Chicago Blackhawks	1934	1961	3
=	New Jersey Devils	1995	2003	3
=	Pittsburgh Penguins	1991	2009	3

*Since the abolition of the challenge match format in 1915; up to and including the 2009 Stanley Cup
Source: NHL

MOST POINTS IN AN NHL CAREER*

	Player	Years	Games	Points
1	Wayne Gretzky	1970–99	1,487	**2,857**
2	Mark Messier	1979–2004	1,756	**1,887**
3	Gordie Howe	1946–80	1,767	**1,850**
4	Ron Francis	1981–2004	1,731	**1,798**
5	Marcel Dionne	1971–89	1,348	**1,771**
6	Steve Yzerman	1983–2006	1,514	**1,755**
7	Mario Lemieux	1984–2006	915	**1,723**
8	Joe Sakic	1988–2009	1,378	**1,641**
9	Jaromir Jagr	1990–2008	1,273	**1,599**
10	Phil Esposito	1963–81	1,282	**1,590**

*Regular season; up to and including the 2008–09 season

Gordie Howe became the first player to achieve 1,000 points when he scored for Detroit in their 2–0 win over Toronto on November 27, 1960. When Wayne Gretzky achieved the same feat on December 19, 1984, he became the 18th to pass the milestone and is the only player to exceed 2,000 points.

MOST PENALTY MINUTES IN AN NHL CAREER*

	Player	Years	Penalty minutes
1	Tiger Williams	1974–88	3,966
2	Dale Hunter	1980–99	3,565
3	Tie Domi	1989–2006	3,515
4	Marty McSorley	1983–2000	3,381
5	Bob Probert	1985–2002	3,300
6	Rob Ray	1989–2004	3,207
7	Craig Berube	1986–2003	3,149
8	Tim Hunter	1981–97	3,146
9	Chris Nilan	1979–92	3,043
10	Rick Tocchet	1984–2002	2,972

*Regular season; up to and including the 2008–09 season

The record by any current player is 2,891 by Chris Chelios between 1983 and 2009. The most penalties in minutes (PIM) in any one season is 472 for Dave Schultz of Philadelphia Flyers in 1974–75. A record 419 penalty minutes were awarded during the Ottawa Senators vs. Philadelphia Flyers match on March 5, 2004.

COACHES IN THE STANLEY CUP*

	Coach	First win	Last win	Total
1	Scotty Bowman	1973	2002	9
2	Toe Blake	1956	1968	8
3	Hap Day	1942	1949	5
4=	Dick Irvin	1932	1953	4
=	Punch Imlach	1962	1967	4
=	Al Arbour	1980	1983	4
=	Glen Sather	1984	1988	4
8=	Pete Green	1920	1923	3
=	Lester Patrick	1925	1933	3
=	Jack Adams	1936	1943	3
=	Tommy Ivan	1950	1954	3

*Since the formation of the NHL in 1917; up to and including 2009

Scotty Bowman's record nine Cup wins came with Montreal Canadiens (5), Detroit Red Wings (3), and Pittsburgh Penguins (1). Toe Blake won a record five consecutive Stanley Cups 1956–60.

MOST RACE WINS IN A FORMULA ONE CAREER BY A DRIVER*

	Driver/country	Years	Wins
1	Michael Schumacher, Germany	1992–2006	91
2	Alain Prost, France	1981–93	51
3	Ayrton Senna, Brazil	1985–93	41
4	Nigel Mansell, UK	1985–94	31
5	Jackie Stewart, UK	1965–73	27
6=	Jim Clark, UK	1962–8	25
=	Niki Lauda, Austria	1974–85	25
8	Juan-Manuel Fangio, Argentina	1950–57	24
9	Nelson Piquet, Brazil	1980–91	23
10	Damon Hill, UK	1993–08	22

*Up to and including the 2009 season

The most career wins by a current driver is 21 by Fernando Alonso (Spain).

LATEST WINNERS OF THE INDY 500 PIT STOP CHALLENGE*

	Team	Driver
2009	Team Penske	Hélio Castroneves
2007	Team Penske	Hélio Castroneves
2006	Team Penske	Hélio Castroneves
2005	Team Penske	Sam Hornish Jr.
2004	Rahal Letterman Racing	Buddy Rice
2003	Cheever Racing	Buddy Rice
2002	Team Penske	Hélio Castroneves
2001	Kelley Racing	Scott Sharp
2000	Panther Racing	Scott Goodyear
1999	Galles Racing	Davey Hamilton

*There was no event in 2008 due to rain

The Pit Stop Challenge is, as its name implies, a pit-stop contest held during the Indy 500 meeting. It has been held since 1977 and takes place on Carb Day. Drivers and their teams simulate pit-stop conditions and the team has to replace four tires and simulate a refuel. Teams compete against each other two at a time, and it is a single elimination contest until there is a winner. Team Penske (formerly Penske Racing) has won the title a record 11 times.

LOWEST STARTING POSITIONS OF WINNERS OF THE INDIANAPOLIS 500*

	Driver	Year	Position
1=	Ray Harroun	1911	28th
=	Louie Meyer	1936	28th
3	Fred Frame	1932	27th
4	Johnny Rutherford	1974	25th
5=	George Souders	1927	22nd
=	Kelly Petillo	1935	22nd
7	Lora Corum/Joe Boyer[†]	1924	21st
8=	Tommy Milton	1921	20th
=	Frank Lockhart	1926	20th
=	Al Unser	1987	20th

*Based on the starting position on the grid; all drivers from the USA
†Joint drivers
Source: Indianapolis Motor Speedway

The winner with the lowest starting grid position since Al Unser's 20th position in 1987 was Eddie Cheever Jr. in 1998, who started from 17th position on the grid.

TOP 10
MOST NASCAR SPRINT
CUP SERIES RACE WINS

	Driver	First win	Last win	Total
1	Richard Petty	1960	1984	**200**
2	David Pearson	1961	1980	**105**
3=	Bobby Allison	1966	1988	**84**
=	Darrell Waltrip	1975	1992	**84**
5	Cale Yarborough	1965	1985	**83**
6	Jeff Gordon[†]	1994	2009	**82**
7	Dale Earnhardt	1979	2000	**76**
8	Rusty Wallace	1986	2004	**55**
9	Lee Petty	1949	1961	**54**
10=	Ned Jarrett	1955	1965	**50**
=	Junior Johnson	1955	1965	**50**

*As of October 17, 2009
†Active in 2009

The Sprint Cup Series is the leading series of races organized by NASCAR (National Association for Stock Car Auto Racing) in the United States. It was known as the Grand National Series between 1950 and 1970, the Winston Cup Series 1971–2003, and the NEXTEL Cup series from 2004 to 2007.

MOTOR SPORTS

TOP 10

MOST WORLD
MOTORCYCLING
GRAND PRIX TITLES*

	Rider/country	Years	Moto GP 500cc	350cc	250cc	125cc	50/80cc	Total
1	Giacomo Agostini, Italy	1966 –75	8	7	0	0	0	15
2	Angel Nieto, Spain	1969 –84	0	0	0	7	6	13
3=	Carlo Ubbiali, Italy	1951 –60	0	0	3	6	0	9
=	Mike Hailwood, UK	1961 –67	4	2	3	0	0	9
=	Valentino Rossi, Italy	1997 –2009	7	0	1	1	0	9
6=	John Surtees, UK	1956 –60	4	3	0	0	0	7
=	Phil Read, UK	1964 –74	2	0	4	1	0	7

	Rider/country	Years	Moto GP 500cc	350cc	250cc	125cc	50/80cc	Total
8=	Geoff Duke, UK	1951 –55	4	2	0	0	0	**6**
=	Jim Redman, Southern Rhodesia	1962 –65	0	4	2	0	0	**6**
10	Anton Mang, West Germany	1980 –87	0	2	3	0	0	**5**
=	Michael Doohan, Australia	1994 –98	5	0	0	0	0	**5**

*Solo classes only; up to and including the 2008 season

MOST MEN'S GRAND SLAM TITLES*

	Player/country	Years	Singles	Doubles	Mixed	Total
1	Roy Emerson, Australia	1959–71	12	16	0	28
2	John Newcombe, Australia	1965–76	7	17	2	26
3=	Frank Sedgman, Australia	1948–52	5	9	8	22
=	Todd Woodbridge, Australia	1988 –2004	0	16	6	22
5	Bill Tilden, USA	1913–30	10	6	5	21
6	Rod Laver, Australia	1960–71	11	6	3	20
7	John Bromwich, Australia	1938–50	2	13	4	19
8=	Jean Borotra, France	1925–36	4	9	5	18
=	Ken Rosewall, Australia	1953–72	8	9	1	18
=	Neale Fraser, Australia	1957–62	3	11	4	18

*Up to and including 2009

John Newcombe's total includes the 1965 Australian Open mixed doubles final, which was not played because of bad weather; the title was shared between the two pairs of finalists.

MOST WOMEN'S GRAND SLAM TITLES*

	Player/country	Years	Singles	Doubles	Mixed	Total
1	Margaret Court (née Smith), Australia	1960–75	24	19	19	**62**
2	Martina Navratilova, Czechoslovakia/USA	1974–2006	18	31	10	**59**
3	Billie Jean King (née Moffitt), USA	1961–81	12	16	11	**39**
4	Margaret Du Pont, USA	1941–62	6	21	10	**37**
5=	Louise Brough, USA	1942–57	6	21	8	**35**
=	Doris Hart, USA	1948–55	6	14	15	**35**
7	Helen Wills-Moody, USA	1923–38	19	9	3	**31**
8	Elizabeth Ryan, USA	1914–34	0	17	9	**26**
9	Steffi Graf, Germany	1987–99	22	1	0	**23**
10	Pam Shriver, USA	1981–87	0	21	1	**22**

*Up to and including 2009

Suzanne Lenglen (France) won 21 Grand Slam events, but if her total of 10 French titles 1920–23 were included, she would appear on this list, but the French Championships up to 1925 were for members of French clubs only, so are not regarded as official Grand Slam events. Elizabeth Ryan also won four French title pre-1925, which would increase her total to 30. Steffi Graf's only doubles title came at Wimbledon in 1988, when she partnered Gabriela Sabatini of Argentina to victory in the women's doubles.

MOST MEN'S SINGLES TITLES*

	Player/country	First win	Last win	Total
1	Jimmy Connors, USA	1972	1989	**109**
2	Ivan Lendl, Czechoslovakia/USA	1980	1993	**94**
3	John McEnroe, USA	1978	1991	**76**
4	Pete Sampras, USA	1990	2002	**64**
5	Guillermo Vilas, Argentina	1973	1983	**62**
6=	Björn Borg, Sweden	1974	1981	**61**
=	Roger Federer, Switzerland	2001	2009	**61**
8	Andre Agassi, USA	1987	2005	**60**
9	Ilie Nastase, Romania	1970	1978	**53**
10	Boris Becker, Germany	1985	1996	**49**

*On the ATP Tour in the Open era 1968–2009
Source: ATP Tour

Connors's first title was in the 1972 Jacksonville Open, when he beat Clark Graebner (USA) 7–5, 6–4.

MOST WOMEN'S SINGLES TITLES*

	Player/country	First win	Last win	Total
1	Martina Navratilova, Czechoslovakia/USA	1974	1994	**167**
2	Chris Evert, USA	1971	1988	**154**
3	Steffi Graf, Germany	1986	1999	**107**
4	Margaret Court (née Smith), Australia	1968	1976	**92**
5	Evonne Cawley (née Goolagong), Australia	1970	1980	**68**
6	Billie Jean King (née Moffitt), USA	1968	1983	**67**
7=	Virginia Wade, UK	1968	1978	**55**
=	Lindsay Davenport, USA	1993	2008	**55**
9	Monica Seles, Yugoslavia/ USA	1989	2002	**53**
10	Martina Hingis, Switzerland	1995	2007	**43**

*On the WTA Tour in the Open era 1968–2009
Source: WTA Tour

FASTEST MEN OVER 100 METERS*

	Athlete/country	Venue	Date	Time (secs)
1	Usain Bolt, Jamaica	Berlin	Aug 16, 2009	9.58
2	Tyson Gay, USA	Berlin	Sep 20, 2009	9.69
3	Asafa Powell, Jamaica	Lausanne	Sep 2, 2008	9.72
4	Maurice Greene, USA	Athens	Jun 16, 1999	9.79
5=	Donovan Bailey, Canada	Atlanta	Jul 27, 1996	9.84
=	Bruny Surin, Canada	Seville	Aug 22, 1999	9.84
7	Leroy Burrell, USA	Lausanne	Jul 6, 1994	9.85
=	Justin Gatlin, USA	Athens	Aug 22, 2004	9.85
=	Olusoji A. Fasuba, Nigeria	Doha	May 12, 2006	9.85
10=	Carl Lewis, USA	Tokyo	Aug 25, 1991	9.86
=	Frank Fredericks, Namibia	Lausanne	Jul 3, 1996	9.86
=	Ato Boldon[†], Trinidad	Walnut	Apr 19, 1998	9.86
=	Francis Obikwelu, Portugal	Athens	Aug 22, 2004	9.86

*Based on the fastest time achieved by each man
†Boldon equaled his personal best mark of 9.86 seconds on three more occasions
Source: IAAF

MOST MEN'S MAJORS IN A CAREER*

	Player/country[†]	Years	Masters	Open	British Open	PGA	Total
1	Jack Nicklaus	1962–86	6	4	3	5	**18**
2	Tiger Woods	1997–2008	4	3	3	4	**14**
3	Walter Hagen	1914–29	0	2	4	5	**11**
4=	Ben Hogan	1946–53	2	4	1	2	**9**
=	Gary Player, South Africa	1959–78	3	1	3	2	**9**
6	Tom Watson	1975–83	2	1	5	0	**8**
7=	Harry Vardon, England	1896–1914	0	1	6	0	**7**
=	Gene Sarazen	1922–35	1	2	1	3	**7**
=	Bobby Jones	1923–30	0	4	3	0	**7**
=	Sam Snead	1942–54	3	0	1	3	**7**
=	Arnold Palmer	1958–64	4	1	2	0	**7**

*Professional Majors only, up to and including 2009
†All golfers from the United States unless otherwise stated

In 1930, Bobby Jones achieved an unprecedented Grand Slam when he won the US and British Open titles as well as the Amateur titles of both countries. Jack Nicklaus, Tiger Woods, Ben Hogan, Gary Player, and Gene Sarazen are the only golfers to have won all four Majors at least once.

MOST TITLES WON ON THE PGA TOUR*

	Player†	Years	Wins
1	Sam Snead	1936–65	82
2	Jack Nicklaus	1962–86	73
3	Tiger Woods	1996–2009	70
4	Ben Hogan	1938–59	64
5	Arnold Palmer	1955–73	62
6	Byron Nelson	1935–51	52
7	Billy Casper	1956–75	51
8	Walter Hagen	1916–36	44
9	Cary Middlecoff	1945–61	40
10=	Gene Sarazen	1922–41	39
=	Tom Watson	1974–98	39

*As of October 18, 2009
†All golfers from the USA

After Tiger Woods, the next best figure by a current player on the Tour is 37 wins by Phil Mickelson

JOCKEYS WITH THE MOST TRIPLE CROWN WINS*

	Jockey/country[†]	Years	Kentucky Derby	Preakness Stakes	Belmont Stakes	Total
1	Eddie Arcaro	1938–57	5	6	6	**17**
2	Bill Shoemaker	1955–86	4	2	5	**11**
3=	Earl Sande	1921–30	3	1	5	**9**
=	Bill Hartack	1956–69	5	3	1	**9**
=	Pat Day	1985–2000	1	5	3	**9**
6=	Jim McLaughlin	1881–88	1	1	6	**8**
=	Gary Stevens	1988–2001	3	2	3	**8**
8=	Charley Kurtsinger	1931–37	2	2	2	**6**
=	Ron Turcotte, Canada	1965–73	2	2	2	**6**
=	Angel Cordero Jr., Puerto Rico	1974–85	3	2	1	**6**
=	Kent Desormeaux	1998–2009	3	2	1	**6**

*Up to and including 2009
†All jockeys from the USA unless otherwise stated

GOLD MEDALISTS AT THE SUMMER X GAMES

	Athlete/country	Sport	Years	Gold medals
1	Dave Mirra, USA	BMX	1996–2005	13
2=	Tony Hawk, USA	Skateboarding	1995–2003	9
=	Travis Pastrana, USA	Moto X/ Rally car racing	1999–2008	9
4	Andy Macdonald, USA	Skateboarding	1996–2002	8
5=	Fabiola da Silva*, Brazil	In-line skating	1996–2007	7
=	Jamie Bestwick, England	BMX	2000–2009	7
7=	Bucky Lasek, USA	Skateboarding	1999–2006	6
=	Bob Burnquist, Brazil	Skateboarding	2001–8	6
9=	Biker Sherlock, USA	Street luge	1996–8	5
=	Rodil de Araujo Jr., Brazil	Skateboarding	1996–2002	5
=	Pierre-Luc Gagnon, Canada	Skateboarding	2002–9	5

*Female competitor

The first ESPN Extreme Games (now X Games) for "alternative" sports were held in June–July 1995. The Games are held every year, and since 1997 there has also been an annual Winter X Games. The events at X Games XV in 2009 were BMX, Moto X, skateboarding, surfing, and rallying. Andy Macdonald holds the overall record with 17 Summer X Games medals.

INDIVIDUAL SPORTS

ACKNOWLEDGMENTS

Richard Braddish

Chris Cole

Paul Dickson

Russell E. Gough

Robert Grant

Anthony Lipmann

Ian Morrison

Dafydd Rees

Robert Senior

Lawrence Shatkin

Academy of Motion Picture Arts and Sciences

Adult Video News

Alexa

Amateur Athletic Union

The American Kennel Club

American Society for Aesthetic Plastic Surgery

Amtrak

artnet

Association of Tennis Professionals

Audit Bureau of Circulations

Box Office Mojo

Breeders' Cup Limited

Centers for Disease Control and Prevention

Central Intelligence Agency

Christie's

ComScore, Inc.

Council on Tall Buildings and Urban Habitat

Death Penalty Information Center

DVD Release Report

Editor and Publisher Yearbook

Emporis

Ethnologue

Euromonitor International

Federal Bureau of Investigation

Food and Agriculture Organization of the United Nations

Forbes

Gold Fields Mineral Services

Golden Raspberry Awards

Hall's Magazine Reports

Imperial War Museum, London, England

Indianapolis Motor Speedway

Institute for Family Enterprise, Bryant College

Interbrand

International Association of Athletics Federations (IAAF)

International Centre for Prison Studies

International Federation of Audit Bureaux of Circulations

International Game Fish Association

International Institute for Strategic Studies

International Obesity Task Force

International Olympic Committee (IOC)

International Shark Attack File, Florida Museum of Natural History

International Telecommunication Union

Internet Movie Database

Internet World Stats
Korbel Champagne Cellars
Lipmann Walton
Magazine Publishers of America
Major League Baseball (MLB)
Miss World
Modern Bride
moviebodycounts.com
Music Information Database
NAACP
National Basketball Association (NBA)
National Center for Education Statistics
National Center for Health Statistics
National Electronic Injury Surveillance System (NEISS)
National Football League (NFL)
National Hockey League (NHL)
National Institute on Alcohol Abuse and Alcoholism
National Insurance Crime Bureau
National Phobics Society
National Public Radio
AC Nielsen
Nielsen Media Research
Online Computer Library Center (OCLC)
Organisation for Economic Co-operation and Development
Organisation Internationale des Constructeurs d'Automobiles
Playboy
Power & Motoryacht
The QSR 50
Recording Industry Association of America (RIAA)
Rolling Stone

Screen Digest
Social Science Quarterly
Social Security Administration
Sotheby's
Stores
United Nations
United Nations Population Division
The United States Army
US Bureau of Labor Statistics
US Census Bureau
US Census Bureau, International Data Base
US Consumer Product Safety Commission
US Department of Agriculture
US Department of Transportation, Federal Highway Administration
US Department of Veterans Affairs
US Geological Survey
US Justice Department
Video Business
Ward's Motor Vehicle Facts & Figures 2009
World Bank
World Gold Council
World Health Organization
World Tennis Association
World Tourism Organization
Yahoo!